I0493777

SECRETS OF INCOME INVESTING

EVERY INVESTOR MUST KNOW ABOUT

ALAN HAFT

Secrets of Income Investing Every

Investor Must Know About

by Alan Haft

Copyright 2014 Alan Haft

ISBN: 978-1497588219

All rights reserved. No part of this publication may be copied, reproduced in any format, by any means, electronic or otherwise, without prior written consent.

The contents of this book are for informational purposes only.

Any product, investment and/or services mentioned in this book may not be suitable for you. If you have any concerns, questions or doubts you should contact an independent financial advisor, licensed tax advisor or licensed legal representative. Some of the investments mentioned may not be regulated under the Financial Services Act 1986 or at all and the protection provided to you under this Act will not apply.

The material in this book does not constitute advice and you should not rely on any material in this book to make (or refrain from making) any decision or take (or refrain from making) any action.

This book (and any of its affiliates) does not make recommendations for buying or selling any securities, options, or insurance products. We make suggestions based on general information and it is up to you to make your own decisions, or to consult with a registered investment advisor, licensed insurance agent, tax advisor, estate planning attorney, or legal representative when evaluating the information in this book.

Alan Haft insurance license OD63810.

ANNUITIES ARE NOT FDIC INSURED, NOT BANK GUARANTEED, MAY LOSE VALUE, INCLUDING LOSS OF PRINCIPAL AND ARE NOT INSURED BY ANY STATE OR FEDERAL AGENCY. ALL INFORMATION IN THIS BOOK SHOULD BE CONSIDERED FOR EXAMPLE AND HYPOTHETICAL ONLY.

TABLE OF CONTENTS

ABOUT THE AUTHOR

Alan Haft is a nationally recognized financial planner and money manager who is often seen on national media such as Fox News network and makes frequent appearances in a wide range of media including CNBC, Money Magazine, The Wall Street Journal, BusinessWeek, USA Today, Forbes, Smart Money and many others. If you're interested in seeing some of Alan's recent television appearances, please visit www.youtube.com/alanhaft.

In addition, Alan has had scores of articles published by the highly prestigious American Institute of Certified Public Accountants (AIPCA) and he is also the author of three books including *The Haft Of It*, *The 10 Most Common Mistakes People Make With Their Money (and how to avoid them)* and his Amazon Top-10 bestseller, *You Can Never Be Too Rich*.

His columns that cover a diverse, wide range of financial subjects have appeared in major newspapers across the country. Furthermore, he has conducted hundreds of simple-to-understand yet highly informative presentations on a wide assortment of financial topics for audiences that range from small groups, local investment clubs, to universities, large conventions and private audiences at venues all across the country at locations such as Donald Trump's Mara Largo.

Previously, Alan was partners with Oscar-nominated actor James Woods in a media company located at Universal Studios and also served as President of Day Corporation, a multi-national technology firm he was instrumental in taking public on the Swiss stock exchange that recently sold to Adobe Corporation.

Contact Alan at alan@alanhaft.com or 800.803.0081

Follow Alan on Twitter @alanhaft

INTRODUCTION

A short while ago, I had the pleasure of meeting someone getting ready to retire from running the finance department at a local car dealership.

Hearing this, instead of diving into retirement income strategies, I quickly turned the tables and asked him questions about his business. What I wanted to know was, "What are the hidden secrets I should know when buying a car? How can one get a good deal and prevent from getting a *bad* one?"

Given he was coming to discuss his retirement income concerns, I didn't want to take too much of his time so I asked for the *Reader's Digest* version.

He cut right to the chase, cleared up much of the confusion, told me *exactly* how it is behind the scenes, what the secrets are as to how one can prevent from getting the short end of the bargain.

After all, when it comes to buying a car, there are many choices out there and because there's just so much information available in the world the more one researches, the more confusing the decision often gets.

When it comes to financial products, I know people share similar anxiety. They will likely do some research, typically hear contradictory opinions, and just as they think they know what they want, they walk into the "financial dealership" where the advisor starts talking in what may as well be a foreign language. Plus, in many cases there's all that fine print. If and when the client dives in, many are left wondering, "What did I just do?"

I know how it feels.

By all means, there was most certainly a time when I didn't understand much about the financial world, its lingo, and the products. I'd hear terminology such as basis points, qualified money, non-qualified money, spreads, collars, and calls and have little or no idea what the person was talking about. The worst part was that underneath the lingo, I just couldn't help feel I wasn't being told everything I needed to know. Even when asked, "Do you have any questions?" not only was I embarrassed by not knowing things I should likely know but more importantly often I didn't even know what questions to ask.

Have you ever felt this way? Believe me, you're not alone, and it's one reason I felt compelled to write this short book. After all, financial confusion exists all over the place.

Take, for example, mutual funds. After doing some research, one might find a fund to invest in but the next step is to then determine whether or not one should invest in *A shares, B shares,* or *C shares.* Brief research on the Internet might unearth a reputable news source advising people against buying *any* of these types of funds and instead advising people to always go into *no load* funds, but then some guy on TV might say that no load funds have higher fees while holding them than loaded funds.

Making matters even more confusing, a few mouse clicks away and there's another expert telling everyone to stay away from *all* mutual funds and go with something called *exchange traded* funds, which seem like mutual funds but they "trade intra-day."

What the heck does that mean?

Yes, at least some level of confusion typically exists all over the place. Today, there are so many different types of investments designed to generate income that you can spend an enormous amount of time researching them and still not scratch the surface of all that's available.

As such, many have turned to advisors, websites, news sources, or friends and chances are they've come across a wide, diverse spectrum of opinions ranging from "(this product) is a great place to put money" to "don't ever put your money into one of those things!"

As a media commentator for mainstream TV networks and national press, I've spent a great deal of time talking to reporters and hosts. In more interviews than I care to remember, I've found highly credible sources combining various products that are far different from one another into *one* product—or worse, completely mistaking one for the other.

Sometimes the information is quite clear, but by the time it trickles down to others, just like the telephone game we played as kids, the message ends up being highly modified. Take, for example, fans of Suze Orman and the subject of annuities. Recently, I was asked to speak at a conference about the power of the exchange traded funds. In the Q&A portion of the event where I often open the floor up to questions about anything, a fan of Suze Orman asked about annuities and proceeded to comment that "Suze *hates* them."

I certainly cannot blame this person given the scrambled eggs nature of information. In fact, in her 2003 book *The Laws of Money, Lessons of Life* Suze clearly advises people to stay far away from *variable* annuities whereas *fixed* annuities are clearly on her list of products she recommends.

If it's even tough for credible news sources to sometimes get the information right, why should it be any easier for you to understand all the products we have at our disposal?

This book is designed to help set the record straight. My intention is to provide what I truly believe is an objective, balanced view of how some of the more common income generating investments work and expose both the potentially positive and potentially negative things one should keep in mind when evaluating these products.

Please keep in mind the purpose of this book is *not* to recommend, defend, or attempt to motivate anyone to stay far away from or hurry into any of the products mentioned in this book. My sole purpose is to deliver what my car friend above provided me: short, concise, simple, and plain English lingo so that in the end you can make much more educated decisions *for yourself* as to whether, "I really need to get (this product)" or "I really need to stay away."

To me, the best use of this book is to read it, hopefully understand it, and then—and only then—begin a journey of closer evaluation during which I firmly believe you'll be much more **empowered** to make the best decision for you, your family, and your hard earned money.

On a final note: I strongly advise reading through the entire book and not skip any sections even if it's not of much interest to you because in many cases, information found in one section will likely be pertinent to understanding concepts found in another part of the book. After all, I tried to keep this book short, to the point and simple, so hopefully you'll agree and manage to speed right through it.

Enough said. Let's begin.

CHAPTER ONE: THE SHIFT TOWARD RETIREMENT

Even if you aren't there yet, you can be certain that at some point in your future you will "retire." Maybe, like quite a few people "in retirement," you might decide to maintain a part time job, not only to earn a few extra dollars but also to keep the mind and body busy as well.

Suffice it to say, either you're there now or one day you will retire and when that time comes, many things in your life will change. The way you eat, the way you play, the things you do... life won't look the same as it did while you were working.

When it comes to investing, many investors' *mindsets* unfortunately don't change as much as they should. In retirement, you are presumably no longer trying to accumulate as much as you used to, rather, many are typically focusing on preserving their money while generating as much *reliable* and *sustainable* income from it. The failure to shift an investment portfolio from the "Accumulation Stage" where one merely wants to grow their money to one designed to generate *reliable returns* leads many people into playing what I call "The Most Dangerous Game."

The Most Dangerous Game

The Most Dangerous Game many people play in retirement is to rely on the *speculative* possibility that their stocks will grow enough to give them the income they need.

And who can blame them? After all, by the time you retire, you've likely just spent many years investing like you did in the previous chapter: purely for *growth*. Such a habit is undoubtedly a bit difficult to break.

All of a sudden, you retire and now need to live off of what you

> The Rule of 100 merely means in order to gain some understanding of how your investment portfolio should be divided between stocks and bonds, merely subtract your age from 100. The result should be the percentage in stocks, the remaining in more conservative investments such as

have. When that happens, no one calls you and says, "Good job and congratulations. You've just retired and now it's time to invest differently." Typically, an investment portfolio gradually and steadily should change over time. Following the Rule of 100 should be doing this for us—as time goes on, we should be reducing our exposure to stocks and increasing our exposure to investments that generate reliable returns such as bonds and other interesting choices I'll soon be discussing. But all too often, especially in the early stages of retirement, the evolution is far too slow, and this is exactly when the Most Dangerous Game's most lethal and devastating train wrecks can take place.

The Story of Dave and Donna

As an example of how an investment portfolio failing to evolve properly can cause train wrecks, let's visit the story of Dave and Donna. Their situation is quite universal, especially for the baby boomers out there.

Back in the last decade, Dave and Donna made a lot of money in the markets, accumulating nearly $2 million in individual stocks. A financial advisor they consulted with assured them they could meet their retirement income goals with "no problem." To keep things simple, their investments needed to generate a 7 percent return to give them the before-tax income they needed, something their advisor assured them he could deliver.

After all, the markets always trend up, don't they? Furthermore, the track record of the managed mutual funds the advisor was suggesting showed impressive rates of return that would certainly provide the income they needed from the potential *growth* of stocks.

Comforted by what they were hearing, and after reviewing the track records of the fund managers, Dave decided to retire.

Over the next year or so, things went fine. Between their individual stocks and stock mutual funds, Dave and Donna were making a substantial enough return to provide them with the income they needed; whatever they pulled out for income was easily being replenished by the continued growth of their stocks.

Making things better, not only was their income being replenished by growth from the stocks, but there was even some excess growth they were reinvesting for future needs.

Everything looked great. The markets were strong, Dave's golf handicap was getting lower by the day, and Donna's tennis game was fantastic. Then, seemingly out of nowhere, the market started taking a turn for the worse.

Thankfully, their investments were somewhat diversified. The advisor had them invested in a scattered few areas of the market, but it was certainly not the type of portfolio that I would truly deem well diversified. However, even with a somewhat diversified portfolio, their investments took a considerable hit, losing roughly 15 percent of their value—which wasn't bad, especially when compared to some other portfolios that fared much worse during those years.

But wait—did they lose only 15 percent? Not exactly. The value of the stocks went down 15 percent, but what else was taking place at the time the market was getting destroyed? From their bathtub of life, at the same time water was going down the drain, they were also removing some of it to live on.

In percentages, they took 7 percent out of their bathtub to live on, but they also lost 15 percent due to water going down the drain, bringing their total loss to 22 percent.

Worried, they consulted with their advisor who, over several occasions, assured them that the professional stock pickers in the mutual funds would "make it back."

With his confidence, they sat tight for another year … and that didn't turn out so well, either. In another bad year, they lost 10 percent of value, plus another 7 percent that they withdrew to cover their income needs.

As the bad markets stabilized, Dave and Donna's portfolio had lost significant value. All it took was two short years to turn what should have been a peaceful retirement into one of great worry and despair. Making matters worse, no thanks to inflation and a few other unforeseen events in their life, by the time the markets finally stabilized, they now needed to generate even *more* income.

When applying this to their portfolio, Dave and Donna had a rude awakening, and, presumably, so did their advisor. Doing the math, it was discovered that with the losses they had suffered, they no longer needed a 7 percent rate of return, but well over a *10 percent rate of return* to give them the income they required.

With well over a 10 percent rate of return needed to provide them with their income, they finally realized they were playing the worst game of all—the gambler's game. Their advisor was relying on the appreciation of their stocks to give them the income they needed, which, as they very quickly learned the hard way, is the Most Dangerous Game to play, during or especially right at retirement.

A client of mine recommended Dave and Donna come see me. Having heard a little about generating reliable returns when in retirement and how to avoid the Most Dangerous Game, they wanted to hear more about investments that were predictable and did not count on the possibility that stocks would always go up in value.

However, as much as we wanted to help them, the damage was already done. Unfortunately, they no longer had the option of repositioning their portfolio into investments that offered reliable returns. Sure, a portion of their portfolio was repositioned to generate more reliable returns. But their need to generate such a high rate of return meant that the majority of their money had to remain heavily invested in the stock markets, keeping their money at risk, albeit in a more diversified portfolio.

As a result of playing the Most Dangerous Game, Dave and Donna no longer have the option their previous advisor once did. Back when Dave retired, if the advisor had simply repositioned portions of the portfolio to produce reliable returns, chances are we wouldn't have met them in the first place.

When evaluating how much income could reliably be generated from their investments, their advisor did not ask himself the single most important question everyone should always ask: What's the worst thing that can happen to this portfolio if things go wrong?

Coming out of the bad market years, I've seen many "Dave and Donnas." The results were not pretty; in fact, some were downright tragic and set many people back years from retirement. Worse, some plans were completely derailed, calling for drastic measures, a change in lifestyle, or even worse.

To sum it up, as far as I'm concerned, this was all caused by their advisor playing the Most Dangerous Game of all: *relying on the speculative appreciation of stocks to provide the income someone needs.*

The Numbers Don't Lie

The following is a conceptual guide one can use to get a very basic idea as to how a portfolio could shift from accumulation to one that offers reliable returns. As previously mentioned, be sure to consult with a qualified advisor before any actions are taken on your investments given everyone's situation will be unique.

With that in mind, here's a few steps to conceptually determine whether repositioning a portfolio into investments that offer reliable returns would make any sense at all. Please note, I am using a before-tax scenario. Because everyone's tax situation is uniquely different, it would be difficult to address all possible variables. For an exact analysis, I urge you to discuss your personal situation with a qualified tax and/or investment advisor:

1. Determine the approximate amount of income you need (expenses, etc.).

2. Reduce this amount by any pension, earnings, or Social Security you receive, or expect to receive.

3. The result represents the dollar amount of income your investments needs to generate.

4. Divide this amount into the total liquid assets you have available (liquid assets would be defined as all investments such as stocks, bonds, IRAs, 401ks, CDs, savings, funds, etc. Liquid assets generally do not include real estate, ownership interests in a company and limited partnerships that are generally

not liquid).

5. To get the decimal in the right place, multiply this amount by 100.

6. The result represents the before-tax *rate of return* the portfolio needs to generate in order to receive the desired income.

To help clarify the above, let's walk through a conceptual example. The numbers and amounts I'm using are obviously greatly simplified just to help you understand the general premise.

Suppose I just retired, I no longer have any earned wages, I am not yet collecting Social Security but I do have a small pension. Using the steps above as my guide, here's how I'd determine an approximate rate of return my investments need to generate in order to provide the income I require:

1. Determine the amount of income needed per year: *as an example, suppose I need a total income of $35,000 dollars per year.*

2. Reduce that amount by any pension, earnings, or Social Security you receive. *As an example, suppose I receive a pension that pays me $12,000 dollars, so the*

$35,000 dollars I need in step one is reduced by the pension.

3. The result represents the amount of income your investments(s) needs to generate. *Therefore, the amount of income my investments need to generate is $23,000 dollars per year ($35,000-$12,000= $23,000 income needed from investments).*

4. Divide this income into the total liquid assets you have available. *Here, I add up all my savings and suppose the amount is $350,000 dollars. I now divide the $23,000 from step 3 into the $350,000 dollars, which equals 0.067.*

5. To get the decimal point in the right place, multiply this by 100. *0.067*100=6.7.*

6. This result represents the before-tax *rate of return* my savings needs to generate in order to get the income I desire.

If the result is a single digit percentage, then you most likely have a good chance of being able to generate reliable income from investments other than stocks. If the result were higher, you may very well find yourself in need of remaining heavily invested in the stock markets. How much you need to keep invested depends on a number of factors.

As an example, one person we recently met wanted to generate as much income as possible from investments that offered reliable rates of return. After a quick analysis, we determined that to get the income he desired, his portfolio would need to generate over a 15 percent return, which is far greater than nearly all return reliable investments offer. In general, the only place to get such a high rate of return for income would be to try getting it from the *speculative* appreciation of stocks. But what does this do? It causes someone to play the Most Dangerous Game.

At such a high return, our advice to this particular individual was: (1) continue striving for higher rates of return in stocks, which would unfortunately keep him playing the Most Dangerous Game; (2) get a part time job to supplement the income reliable returns can comfortably generate; (3) reduce expenses; (4) delay retirement a few years; and/or if none of these choices are possible, (5) downsize to a smaller residence (to free up more money) or refinance some equity in his house, which comes with its own set of issues too complex to address here.

Needless to say, at such a high-required rate of return, this person did not have the option of peacefully repositioning investments from his accumulation stage portfolio into investments that generate reliable returns for income, as Dave and Donna once did.

So, if you are like Dave and Donna and you *have* the opportunity they once did to reposition portions of the investments into ones that efficiently produce reliable returns, this could easily be the most important section in this book.

Let's continue.

How to Avoid the Most Dangerous Game

As simplistic as it sounds, Dave and Donna's problem could have been completely avoided.

The problem was that when the time came for them to generate income from their accounts, their advisor did not reposition any of their portfolio into investments to produce reliable income, defined as: *a rate of return one can generally rely on regardless if the value of stocks in a portfolio goes up or down.*

Especially when it comes to producing income, the first consideration should be to use the safest and the most reliable investments—investments that, as much as possible, do not rely on the speculative possibility that stocks might go up in value. Plain and simple, relying on the growth of stocks to generate the income one needs is just downright *un*reliable, no matter how well the markets are currently performing or how appealing a stock picker's track record appears.

A mind-set that prevents a shift from the accumulation stage to the reliable return stage is often that of an investor that believes the stock markets go nowhere but up or a tax-conscious investor. Many people gravitating toward retirement hesitate to sell stocks that have appreciated quite well because they don't want to pay the capital gains tax. Even though they can reposition their assets to go into investments that will create more reliable bird in the hand returns, they simply won't do it because they'll have to pay tax.

My gosh. Do you know how many people we met coming off the highs of the late 1990s who would give their right arm and left leg to be able to turn back the clock, sell some growth, pay the tax, and invest in reliable income-producing investments?

Sometimes paying the tax on growth stocks, especially at retirement, would be the *best* deal you could ever find.

So, what are the investments out there that provide reliable returns? There are quite a few, some of which I'll be discussing in this important chapter. But before going any further, let's make sure we're clear on what a "reliable return is:

The reliable return investments I'm talking about can be as simplistic as bank certificates of deposit (CDs). Certainly there are many other investments that produce considerably higher rates of reliable return that I'll soon be discussing, but a CD does provide a rate of return that is reliable. The return will be there regardless of whether or not the stock portion of the diversified portfolio goes up or down in value.

If I have $100,000 in CDs paying me 5 percent (attractive at the time of this writing), then the $5,000 of interest is a return that I can safely rely on, regardless of how my stocks perform. This return is totally and completely independent of the value of my stocks. Of course, for a variety of reasons I'll be discussing, it certainly wouldn't be prudent for most people to invest a large portion of their money in CDs. Coming up, we will soon see there are many other investments that can generate significantly higher reliable rates of return and opportunity for growth as well, but for now, I'm using the lowly CD just to illustrate the point.

I cannot stress it enough: When it comes to avoiding the Most Dangerous Game, the return an investment portfolio generates must *not* rely on stocks going up in value. As much as possible, to avoid the Most Dangerous

Game, reliable returns needs to exist in the portfolio, especially in the worst-case scenarios.

Are You Playing the Most Dangerous Game?

Are you getting close to retirement? Are you already there? Do you know whether or not you are playing the Most Dangerous Game? Most people have no idea, and as of this very moment, that's okay. You're reading this book and I'm working to help you figure it out.

If you are nearing retirement or are in it, one of the quickest ways to give you a preliminary idea as to how much you are currently relying on the speculative growth of stocks to generate the income you need is to take a look at your brokerage statements. These statements generally provide much of the information you need.

Each brokerage statement, especially if issued by one of the larger firms, typically has a line item, often on the first page or in the back summary, that reports the total annual income a portfolio generates from something called dividends and interest. This line item typically is separate from the *value* of your stocks.

Often, this will be stated as a dollar figure.

In Dave and Donna's case, a quick look at their statements revealed the total income their investments were generating was $20,000 (through dividends and interest). This $20,000 represented the reliable return their portfolio was generating that did not depend on the speculative growth of their stocks. This $20,000 return was *separate* from their stocks going up or down in value. It's a very important distinction to make and it cannot be emphasized enough.

Regardless of whether the value of their stocks went up or down, this $20,000 should generally remain constant. In their case, it was the only reliable return within their portfolio—everything else was based on the pure speculation of stocks growing in value. This reliable return represented dividends and interest from their portfolio, and this amount was completely independent from the value of their stocks.

If it sounds a bit confusing, stay with me. It's about to hopefully get clearer.

The $20,000 of dividends and interest (the reliable return) in Dave and Donna's investments represented a 1 percent return on the entire portfolio of investments. The return their portfolio was producing, separate from the possibility of growth, was simply 1 percent, when in fact they initially needed 7 percent. Therefore, the 6 percent they needed *above* this 1 percent *might* come from one place and one place only: the *possibility* that their stocks would increase in value, a possibility that Dave and Donna learned the hard way is not guaranteed by any means, regardless of how impressive the mutual fund manager's track record first appeared. As the old saying goes, "Past performance does not guarantee future results," and in Dave and Donna's unfortunate case, that couldn't have been closer to the truth.

Investors withdrawing money from a stock portfolio could mistakenly believe their investments are doing just fine. In Dave and Donna's case, if they received over 7 percent on their investments it could *appear* the portfolio is reliably producing the income they need. However, without carefully evaluating the *reliable* return portion of their portfolio, they eventually got a nasty surprise the moment their stocks did not perform well.

Therefore, to avoid playing the Most Dangerous Game, one should strongly consider repositioning enough of their accumulation assets into investments that generate reliable returns. With enough accumulation assets repositioned into investments that offer reliable returns, ideally, the "total income" line item found on a brokerage statement would be *at least equal* to the amount of income one needs. In the prior example of the man needing over a 15 percent return on his investments in order to provide him with the income he needs, this is not always possible by any means.

A Simple Demonstration of Repositioning Assets for Reliable Income

I'm going to be extremely simplistic about this, but it does help clarify the point. I'm going to walk you through a conceptual restructuring of a portfolio that is in the accumulation stage and now needs to generate reliable returns for income.

Suppose I just retired and I have a total nest egg of $200,000 worth of growth stocks.

Now retired, I need to generate income from my investments. If I kept my $200,000 in growth stocks and I start drawing income, I'm playing the Most Dangerous Game. Why? Because I am relying on the possibility that my stocks will go up in value to provide me with the income I need.

To avoid the Most Dangerous Game, I am going to first evaluate my income needs and then apply this amount to my current investments. Going through this exercise will help me conceptually determine if I am playing the Most Dangerous Game.

So, going back to the steps outlined earlier, I first need to figure out the total income I need for the year, which I decide is (a low figure for simple math) $7,000 before-tax.

Checking my portfolio, I see I am playing The Most Dangerous Game - my money is invested all in growth stocks that produce very little income. To learn this, all I did was look at my statement; I found the area that shows me the total income (dividends and interest) for the year.

In this hypothetical example, the total dividends and interest is quite low, revealing the entire portfolio is most likely invested in pure growth stocks that produce little income (which, by the way, is generally true of many growth stock indexes one might use in a diversified portfolio as described in the previous sections). Yes, if the stocks increase in value more than what I withdraw, then I am doing fine. I am not accelerating losses nor am I chipping away at my principal. But relying on the speculative growth of the stocks to generate the income I need is what someone playing the Most Dangerous Game does. And remember: Whether in the accumulation stage or in the reliable returns stage, we do not want to gamble; we want to be investors and leave as little to chance as possible.

In Dave and Donna's case, their advisor was working with the belief that the speculative growth of stocks would easily provide the income they need. Over time, I would certainly endorse this belief. But as one gets close to retirement, one rarely has much time to make up a loss. As mentioned, the advisor was not asking, "What's the worst thing that can happen to this portfolio?" He was not telling himself, "If a bad market causes a loss of value and the investor is withdrawing money they need for income at the same time, then overall losses would be accelerated." I like to compare this to that bathtub of water: If you are withdrawing water to live on, God forbid the drain is left open at the same time.

So, instead of relying on the speculative growth of stocks to provide me with the income I need, a far better approach would be to reallocate enough of the $200,000 into investments that offer reliable returns. How much do I need to reallocate? The answer comes down to how much income I need, tax considerations that of course need to be factored in, and the returns currently available in the arena of reliable income producing investments.

After evaluating the marketplace for investments that can generate a reliable return, my advisor and I determine that we can count on receiving 7 percent on our money.

Next step: I then need to re-position enough of my growth stocks into investments that generate the before-tax income I require. Simple math tells me if I need $7,000 to produce the before-tax income I require and investments that offer reliable returns currently offer 7 percent, then I'd need to fund the portfolio of reliable investments with $100,000 ($100,000 generating 7 percent equals $7,000 for my income).

The amount leftover that I do *not* use to produce my income should generally remain in a diversified *stock* portfolio for growth. If the leftover amount does not grow in value, my income will not be affected, nor will I *accelerate* the loss by drawing money from this area, as Dave and Donna's advisor unfortunately did. Remember them? Their account lost 22 percent of its value because they withdrew 7 percent from the same "pot" of money that lost 15 percent.

Bottom line: by keeping reliable income-producing investments *separate* from stock investments striving for growth, one now avoids playing the Most Dangerous Game.

As time goes by and the stock portion of my investments presumably goes up in value, when I need more income to compensate for things such as inflation, I merely *shift* money from the diversified stock portfolio over into investments that are providing me with the reliable returns. Doing so will naturally increase my income.

So, what have I essentially done here?

After repositioning investments from growth stocks to investments that offer reliable returns, when I look at my brokerage statement I *now* see my "total income" (dividends and interest) is *equal* to my target income of $7,000 per year.

Receiving this income does not rely on the *possibility* that my stocks will go up in value. From various investments we'll soon discuss, this 7 percent return will generally be there regardless of whether or not my stocks go up or down in value. I have successfully *separated* the income I need from the speculative possibility that my stocks will go up in value.

If this all sounds a bit too simplistic, you might be very surprised at some of the things that I have seen; there are many out there still relying *only* on the *possible* growth of stocks to give them the income they need. That is what the Most Dangerous Game is all about, and I hope you now have a conceptual understanding of how to avoid it. *If you are approaching or are in retirement, this will likely be the most important lesson this book has to offer.*

Now that you've learned a few things about the Most Dangerous Game, don't be afraid to speak up and ask questions. It is *your* money in your portfolio; you obviously have every right to evaluate the methods being used to produce the income you need. A year or two after a dip in the stock market is *not* the right time to stop playing the

Most Dangerous Game. At that point in time, it could be too late to make changes for the better.

The best time to shift from playing the Most Dangerous Game is *before* the time when you need to generate reliable returns. So, even if a growth portfolio is doing fantastic, be sure to remember the Most Difficult Investment Formula In The World: Investing - Emotion = Success.

Fund manager on a tear? Stocks surging in value? Taxes to be paid if you make the shift from speculation to reliability? It doesn't matter to me. Someone can tell me all day long that his or her stocks are "doing great." I have heard this a thousand times, but it makes little difference to me. I've seen the destruction one bad market can cause, and God forbid it happens to you. After all, this is money you've most likely worked real hard for, isn't it? It would certainly be a total shame if it was lost due to playing the Most Dangerous Game when it may never had to have been played at all.

When it comes to my money, with the exception of the portion placed in my flavors of the day, I am not a speculator. I am an investor, and you should be too. Few people get rich by *hoping* to make money in the market. Rich people get wealthy by being smart. They get rich by taking action and anticipating future events such as the need to soon or now need to start generating income; as Wayne Gretzky often said, "Skate to where the puck is going, not where it currently is."

Need income? Speculating on the possibility that the value of your stocks *might* increase enough in value to generate the precious income you need? Don't experience what Dave and Donna did. Always ask the question, "What's the worst thing that can happen here?" If the worst thing that can happen is that you are playing the Most Dangerous Game and need to soon or now start generating income, begin making transitions now. Don't wait. Take the profits, pay the tax, do whatever it takes to get into more reliable investments. Let the speculators out there live through the uncertainty of the markets.

This is your life we're talking about, remember?

Stock Market Stan Teaches Us a Lesson

Until this point, I've discussed people such as Dave and Donna who once had the opportunity to reposition portions of their portfolio into safer, more reliable income-producing investments. But at the beginning of this chapter, I mentioned that reliable return strategies are not just for the retired person looking to generate income, but for the investor merely seeking growth as well.

As mentioned, investments that offer reliable returns not only generate income, but they also can help buffer bad markets. If stocks go down in value, then the money allocated to reliable return investments can at least offer some return for the overall portfolio.

In some cases, investing the majority of a portfolio into investments that offer *only* reliable returns even when income is not the priority can make sense as well. To illustrate the point, a person I will call "Stock Market Stan" provides a great example.

Stock Market Stan is one of those individuals who really doesn't have much of a reason to be in the stock market at all. Relative to the value of his nest egg, the returns he can safely generate from reliable investments will provide him with more returns than he'll ever need.

Now, your first inclination might be that I'm referring to people who have amassed a lot of money. But that isn't always the case. I've met many people who could be construed as having just a little bit of money. But given that they need so little income from their investments, in some cases, there are many people who can afford to keep the majority of their nest egg in investments that offer reliable returns.

We often find many people who need very little income remain very heavily invested in the stock markets. Chances are they are still heavily invested in stocks for any one of the following reasons: They know of no other way to invest, they believe the markets will always go up, old habits are hard to break, greed, or the plain old-fashioned love of the action.

Any one of these reasons can certainly be valid. After all, it's not my life, nor is it my money, and as a result, who am I to judge? But that said, many people out there *do* want to know if there's a better or safer way; they are open to hearing or want other ideas, and perhaps learning a few things about Stock Market Stan could help.

Stock Market Stan

When I first met him, Stock Market Stan just turned 60. Over the years, he's managed to do a fantastic job for he and his wife. Thanks to the sale of a business, he amassed an investment portfolio of well over $5 million. Now, before I proceed, keep in mind: While over $5 million is certainly a lot of money, this same scenario can easily apply to someone with less money, especially if they are well into retirement. Relatively speaking, it's the percentages that count most, not the dollar amounts.

From Stock Market Stan's $5 million-plus portfolio, thanks to various real estate holdings outside this portfolio, he and his wife withdraw very little from their investments. In percentages, Stan's portfolio needs to generate less than 1 percent return each year to produce the occasional income they require.

Stock Market Stan came in one day wanting to hear some thoughts on how to leave more money to his kids. After learning a few things about he and his wife, I asked how much of their money was invested in stocks, he replied, "Most of it." I asked why someone with over $5 million dollars, needing less than a 1 percent rate of return to cover occasional cash flow needs would need to be so heavily invested in stocks. He couldn't really answer the question; an advisor up north was managing his investments.

My response to Stan: after consideration to taxes, sell most of the stocks and make the majority of the money safe. Want to leave more money to the kids? For reasons I'll later discuss, maybe consider investing a small amount into an insurance policy. As for the rest of the money, invest it in high quality municipal bonds and other safe investments that offer reliable returns.

With the reliable returns these investments produce, the tax-free interest they produce would far exceed his occasional income requirement. From this reliable return, withdraw the occasional income he needs and as for the remaining amount, use *that* money to invest in stocks. Worst-case scenario, some of the stocks go down in value. But the following year, the cycle repeats. The nest egg will always be there, and so will his reliable returns that provide not only his occasional income needs, but new money to invest in stocks as well.

While repositioning the majority of his portfolio into safer, reliable investments might sound like a radical idea, in their interviews with the *New York Times*, this is exactly what people such as former Fed Chairman Alan Greenspan and Suze Orman mentioned they do. And please, don't always assume this is only for the "rich people." As stated before, the same rules can apply to anyone—it's not always about the dollar amount of the portfolio; it's much more about the portfolio relative to who the person is and what he or she needs it to accomplish.

In her *New York Times* interview, Suze Orman stated her net worth is somewhere around $30 million. If she generates 5 percent returns from safe investments such as municipal bonds (which is where she said she invests most of her money), that's $1.5 million per year in reliable returns.

Can she live off that $1.5 million? Probably. Can she gamble that $1.5 million and lose it all in the markets? Sure, because she knows her $30 million is completely safe and it will always be there next year, and the year after that, and the year after that.

And what about Carole Smith? Carole is a friend of ours in her 80s. Not including her house, she has a total net worth of $250,000. Her pension and Social Security provide her with more income than she needs, and her health care expenses are well taken care of thanks to a rock-solid government plan. Requiring no income from her portfolio, wouldn't it be prudent to reposition much of her individual stock portfolio into investments that provide safe and reliable returns? Carole agreed, and as a result, she decided to reposition much of her portfolio into investments that provide reliable returns. The most important result, however, is that Carole now leads a far less stressful investment life that doesn't require her to panic every time the stock market has a problem.

After learning about Carole, Suze, and Stock Market Stan, if you can afford it, perhaps you will consider doing the same for large, medium or small portions of your investments. Bottom line: If you don't need the *potential* return, why take the risk?

Where Do You Fit In?

So, where do you fall in the investment spectrum? Are you a Stock Market Stan who can afford to place most of your money to investments that offer reliable returns?

Or are you a Dave and Donna, newly retired, who could have benefited from balancing between stocks and investments that offer reliable rates of return to generate the income they need?

Many people nearing or entering retirement—especially the baby boomers—are finding themselves a bit short of where they need to be. They simply cannot afford to put their investments into the safest things possible, given that they don't have the luxury of the Stans, Suzes, and Caroles of the world who could generate more return than they'll ever need from reliable investments.

For some people, realizing their goals might not be as easily attainable as they once thought (and there are no doubt a lot of people out there like this). Therefore, generating reliable returns poses its own set of unique challenges.

Getting Away from the Most Dangerous Game

Let's go back to baby boomers Dave and Donna.

If you recall, Dave and Donna calculated their annual income needs and with the help of an advisor, determined they would need a 7 percent rate of return on their investments to maintain their lifestyle. However, they were playing the Most Dangerous Game, because their advisor believed getting a 7 percent return in the markets was easy. As they learned the hard way, only 1 percent of that return was being generated from reliable investments.

The additional 6 percent needed for their income was coming from the *speculative possibility* that their stocks would increase in value, which unfortunately just did not happen.

This Most Dangerous Game is one played by far too many investors and advisors who seem to have too much trust in the market's appreciation. In the long term, I would absolutely agree that the markets *should* provide a return of 7 percent or better to get Dave and Donna the income they needed. But when in retirement, or approaching it, "the long term" certainly won't help if things go bad, as we witnessed in Dave and Donna's case. If things go bad, there quite simply won't be enough time to recover the loss.

No one wants to lose money. But if you are going to take a loss, it's certainly better to do so when you are working and accumulating money during those years. In these cases, you, a fund manager, or I can afford to recover or make up a few losses along the way. However, in retirement (especially during the early stages) it's a totally different story. All it took to start Dave and Donna's perpetual downward spiral was two short years.

As I've stated, for people like Dave and Donna, or others who need to generate income from their investments, counting on the speculative growth of stocks to deliver the return is the Most Dangerous Game.

This statement, I'm sure, can leave you wondering, "Okay, so can I generate *reliable* income from my investment portfolio, while at the same time, especially during the early years of retirement, *also* grow my money?"

Challenging? Not exactly. There are a few key places to invest that are much more reliable than the possibility of stocks growing in value to generate the income one needs. And there are also investments that can give you the potential for both: reliable returns for income and the possibility for growth. It may at first sound like magic, but I can assure you, it's really not.

The following possibilities are some of my favorite investments that offer reliable returns, but by no means are they the only choices out there.

Bear in mind that to generate reliable returns, this group of investment types is not intended as a "pick one and run with it" kind of deal. Typically, a reliable return portfolio should consist of a diversified *combination* of investments that follow, and perhaps some that are not mentioned here. So, when it comes to generating reliable returns that do not rely on the speculative growth of stocks to provide the income one needs, here are a few possibilities that can get the job done.

Dividend Stocks

Dividends are cash payments from stocks; they are often used to generate income and can be an excellent way to get both income and the possibility of growth. Dividends can change and are not guaranteed. At any time, without warning, a company may even eliminate them, but we are going to learn some ways to minimize this risk. Receiving dividends while at the same time having the possibility of growth is a particularly strong strategy for many baby boomers who generally need both things at the same time: income and growth from their investments.

Bonds

Bonds have a stated rate of return—a "bird in the hand." For example, a bond may pay you 7 percent on your investment. That's a bird in the hand. When you invest in a bond, you know the return you'll get. Furthermore, investment grade (good quality) bonds typically ensure that your money is safe. The downside to bonds is that they generally offer little growth, if any. If you are deep into retirement, it may make sense to have most of your money in bonds, but most of us moving toward retirement or are in the early stages of it should certainly not rely on this one instrument alone.

CDs

Have you heard about CDs that could pay greater than 10 percent? We'll soon be exploring these interesting investments many have not heard of.

Real Estate Investment Trusts

A REIT is a security that invests directly in real estate, either through properties or mortgages. You can buy or sell a REIT just like you would a stock on the major stock exchanges. I'll be making a few comments about these coming up.

Preferred Stocks

This hybrid of a stock and a bond often appears in investment engines designed to generate income. Because they are so often used, I'll give a quick description of what they are. However, I won't spend as much time on them as

I will with the other choices given something I refer to as the "heads I win, tails you lose" nature of some preferred stocks.

Annuities

These contracts offered by insurance companies are specifically designed for those moving closer to, or are already in retirement, especially during the initial years of it. Annuities offer some benefits that cannot be found anywhere else and given much confusion about them, I'll end this book with an entire section devoted to just how they work.

Let's take a look at each possibility above and more in greater detail.

CHAPTER TWO: DIVIDEND STOCKS

Most people would be inclined to think the following scenario cannot be possible, but by the end of this chapter, I'll show you how it's done. No, it's not one of David Copperfield's magic tricks. The only magic is what dividend stocks can do for you.

Suppose I invest $100,000 in a diversified portfolio of dividend stocks.

From the outset, the dividend stock portfolio generates $7,000 per year in reliable income (that's a 7 percent return, and yes, it can be done—I'll show you where in a little while).

Every investor's worst fear comes true: The stock markets get hit real hard; the value of the dividend stock portfolio goes down 30 percent and is now worth $70,000.

With the portfolio of stocks now worth far less of what it was worth when I started, how much income can the portfolio reliably produce now?

Answer: the *same* $7,000 the portfolio produced before the value went down.

Strange? Absolutely. True? Without a doubt. Guaranteed? Not at all, but I will show you how to reduce the risk.

During the rest of this very important section, we'll learn many of the ins and outs of dividend stocks, the risks and the rewards as to how in the worst-case scenario, your portfolio can still potentially produce a highly attractive and reliable rate of return.

When it comes to generating reliable returns from your money, especially for the baby boomers out there, discussing dividend stocks is often my favorite subject of all.

For those of you who have not heard of these things call dividends, some stocks pay dividends, and the ones that do offer the best of many possible worlds:

- Possibility of growth
- Income
- Free stocks

Regardless of whether you are investing for growth, for income, or to receive free stocks, here's a quote that does a pretty good job of summarizing just how important dividend stocks are to every investor: "Dividends have accounted for well over half of the long-term real return on big-company stocks."—*Forbes*, June 7, 2004.

Take dividends out of the equation, and the growth one can potentially receive in the stock markets certainly doesn't look as appealing as it once did.

Dividends Defined

In its most simplistic form, a dividend is a cash payment made to the shareholder of a company. As an example, if I own one share of stock of ABC Company and ABC pays a cash dividend of $1 for each share I own, then logically, when ABC pays a cash dividend to its shareholders I would get $1.

Now, here is a very crucial point that we will be exploring in greater detail:

The $1 cash dividend I receive from owning my one share is totally *independent* from the *market value* of the stock itself. For purposes of this section, this is such an important point that I need to repeat it: *The $1 dividend I receive from owning my one share is independent from its value.*

Let's make sure you understand it by way of an example: Assume I own one share of ABC Company stock.

- If ABC Company stock is valued at $10 per share and ABC pays a dividend of $1 per share, how much cash do I receive? $1, right? Right!
- If ABC Company stock goes *down* in value from $10 to $5 per share, and ABC pays a dividend of $1 per share, how much cash do I receive? $1, right? Right!
- What happens if my one share of ABC Company goes *up* in value, and what once was worth $10 per share turns into another Berkshire Hathaway? If ABC stock is valued at $100,000 per share and ABC pays a dividend of $1 per share, how much income do I receive? $1, right? Right!

As you can see in these examples, the amount of income (dividend) the company pays per share has *nothing* to do with the market value of the share. Therefore, the cash I receive is based on the *amount*, or the *quantity* of shares I own, *not* the value of them.

Bottom line: when it comes to generating reliable returns from stocks that pay dividends, the value of the stock is totally independent from the dividend I receive.

You may want to read the preceding paragraph a few times until it sticks with you. If you remember and understand it, "magic" will happen. This magic is most valuable when you need to generate *income* and the possibility of *growth* from your portfolio.

To see how powerful this can be, let's start by taking one big step back.

A Closer Look at Dividends

Most investors are somewhat familiar with stock market investing. Each share of stock you hold represents a portion of actual ownership in a company. As a large or even small stockholder, you stand to gain or lose money based on how that company performs.

But when it comes to understanding the value of dividends, one of the first things you need to completely understand is that a stock can make you money one of two possible ways: by appreciating in value or by generating cash in the form of dividends.

Most people are only familiar with making money in stocks when they go up in value. But that only represents one way returns can be generated. On the other side of the fence, generating cash in the form of dividends tends to be vastly underrated. After all, when a dividend is paid, you literally get *cash* paid into your account, and that's obviously not such a bad thing. Given how attractive this could be, I'd like to take some time to discuss this very important area of investing to build wealth or to generate reliable returns for income from this type of stock.

When a company makes a profit, at the company's discretion, a portion of the earnings can be distributed to its stockholders in the form of cash. The distribution is called a dividend. Although there are many reasons a company might distribute a dividend, one of the main reasons is that it's a way for the company to reduce taxes.

Dividends are typically paid by large companies that generate regular profits but are too mature to grow significantly. Examples of such companies are General Electric and Coca-Cola. Fast-growing companies in new industries such as telecommunications and biotechnology seldom pay dividends. Instead, they reinvest their profits to help grow the company.

Prior to the bull market of the 1990s, the average dividend yield on stocks in the Standard & Poor's (S&P) 500 index was about 4 percent. During the 1990s, however, dividends declined as many companies reinvested their profits in an attempt to generate much-desired growth. By the time the bull market ended in 2000, according to *Smart Money* magazine (October 7, 2002, Internet edition), the average dividend yield on stocks in the S&P 500 had declined to 1.5 percent. In 2003, thanks to something called the Jobs and Growth Tax Relief Reconciliation Act, special tax incentives for corporations made distributing dividends quite attractive.

In the past, dividends were taxed more heavily, much to the disappointment of many investors, who argued that this amounted to double taxation—a company was taxed on its profits and then shareholders receiving dividends were taxed on those same profits as well. The Jobs and Growth Tax Relief Reconciliation Act dramatically cut the federal tax rate on stock dividends from a maximum of 38.6 percent down to 15 percent, and as a result many companies began increasing their dividends. For example, in 2004, Microsoft made a special $32 billion one-time dividend payment of $3 per share and doubled its regular dividend to 32 cents per share.

This change in the tax law makes dividend-paying stocks particularly attractive to income-seeking investors as an income-producing option, as well as to growth investors looking to ensure a portion of their individual stocks have something to show for taking risk via receiving the cash these stocks produce.

In addition, dividends paid to an investor can also be reinvested to acquire more shares of the company that just issued the dividend itself. Instead of receiving the dividend as cash, the dividend is reinvested to purchase more shares.

Some refer to this as "receiving free shares of stock," given that you are using the cash the company pays in the form of a dividend to buy additional shares.

Contrary to some opinions, you don't need to always worry that dividend-paying stocks produce cash but have little chance for appreciation. If you take a look at the dividend-paying stocks in the S&P 500, they had an average return of 28 percent in 2003, the year the Jobs and Growth Tax Relief Reconciliation Act was introduced. By no means does the fact a company pays dividends mean the growth will always be stagnant when compared to companies that pay no dividends.

With dividend stocks, you get the best of both possible worlds: income *and* growth. However, while this all may sound good, there are most certainly risks. A company can *cut* a dividend at any time. While some companies have long track records of rarely, if ever, missing a dividend payment, it could happen without notice. And when relying on the dividends being paid for income, a missing dividend would not be very reliable thing, would it?

To minimize the risk, when needing to rely on dividends for income, I often recommend staying away from investing in individual dividend-paying stocks. Relying on individual stocks to pay dividends can be a dangerous and unreliable proposition, something we definitely want to avoid as much as possible.

Let's take a closer look.

The Danger of Individual Dividend Stocks

Years ago, a company known as NovaStar has not performed well. I don't mean to pick on NovaStar, but what happened to this company demonstrates the danger of relying on individual stocks to pay dividends, especially for those looking to generate reliable returns for income, such as a retired investor who needs a predictable cash flow.

For the past several years, NovaStar was a bright, shining star of the dividend world, paying an attractive dividend. One day, however, NovaStar announced the company was having problems and needed to retain more of its capital. So what did it do? It made an unexpected decision to no longer pay dividends to its shareholders.

What do you think happened to the value of the stock? As soon as the announcement came out, the value of the stock tanked. Investors not only lost their shirts, but some lost their pants, shoes, and underwear as well.

The same thing happened to a company known as Impac Holdings. For years, it paid an attractive dividend as well. It was the staple and mainstay of many investment portfolios looking to generate income from dividend stocks, and for quite a while, it was doing really well for its investors. Then, one dark, unpleasant day, the dividend was drastically reduced. As a result, the value of the stock dropped considerably. Not only was the once reliable income cut, but the value of the stock went way down.

Not good.

Because companies can cut or even eliminate the dividends (income) they pay to the stockholders at any time, receiving dividend income from individual stocks cannot be considered highly reliable by any means. There are some companies out there that over the course of decades have not missed a dividend payment, but this does not mean that they never will.

As with any investment, as I've mentioned many times before, one must always ask the question, "What's the worst thing that could happen here?" With dividend stocks, the worst thing that can happen is what happened to those who owned stock in NovaStar or Impac; the dividend is eliminated, the stock loses a great deal of value, and someone starts tossing unreliable financial advisors out windows.

That's a pretty bad worst-case scenario.

But wait … haven't I introduced you to dividend stocks as a *reliable* way to produce *consistent* returns? Yes, I have. So let's explore the way to minimize the risks I've just mentioned.

Avoiding the Pitfalls of Individual Dividend Stocks

The best way to protect against the type of disaster where a company cuts a dividend and its stock value plummets is, as always, *diversify*. When investing in dividend stocks for reliable returns and the possibility for growth, one can purchase many dividend stocks in a variety of diversified market sectors. That is one way of creating reliable returns.

If one of your many dividend stocks suddenly stops paying a dividend, you are reducing risk by the fact that in a diversified dividend stock portfolio, you wouldn't have a large percentage of your overall investment in any one place.

Sounds good, but we're not out of the woods yet. Diversification among many dividend-paying stocks certainly helps, but there are still a few problems we need to address.

First is the expense of diversifying. If you wanted to diversify your portfolio by purchasing a large number of individual dividend-paying stocks, the trading costs alone would not be attractive and would reduce your overall return.

Second, having to keep track of all of these stocks can be quite cumbersome.

Third, and most important, having to choose which dividend stocks to invest in can be very time-consuming.

There is a better answer, and the answer is to consider diversifying your money in a mutual fund, an exchange-traded fund, or something called a "closed-end mutual fund."

Using Closed-End Funds to Generate Dividends

One possibility to create a portfolio of diversified dividend stocks is by investing in exchange traded funds or closed-end mutual fund. Given I spent significant time discussing exchange traded funds in the previous chapter, I'll focus my attention here on the closed-end mutual fund. For simplicity, a closed-end mutual fund on a brokerage statement at first appears to trade and act similar to the way an individual stock does. But while on a brokerage statement it might at first look like it's one stock, in reality, it's not even close.

That "one stock" (the closed-end fund) can easily have hundreds if not thousands of stocks inside it. Furthermore, the value of a closed-end fund is based on supply and demand, whereas its closely related cousin, the open-ended mutual fund, determines its value based on what is known as the net asset value, which simply means the value of the stocks in the fund.

Let's imagine we're back at the casino I described earlier, and let's return to a roulette table where the numbers on the table all represent stocks that pay dividends. Instead of picking one number such as black 25 (an individual dividend stock), through a closed-end fund you are automatically invested in *many* numbers on the table. On this "dividend stock roulette table," all of the numbers pay dividends, so if one number winds up not performing well like NovaStar, you're not going to be hurt as much as you would be if you owned it individually. NovaStar might have stopped paying a dividend, potentially sending the value of the company's stock into the toilet, but the damage to your game is considerably less, given that this stock is just one of many other stocks that can much better sustain the overall dividend payments, therefore making the income much more reliable.

Some roulette tables consisting of dividend stocks inside a closed-end fund pay attractive dividends—in some cases anywhere from 4 to 10 percent, sometimes even higher. Furthermore, many closed-end funds pay these dividends consistently, typically on a monthly basis.

The risk of these funds is that while the *income* may be generally reliable, it's possible for the *value* of the portfolio to not only go up, but to possibly go down as well. After all, these are stocks we're talking about, not CDs. This brings us to a very important point. Investors who cannot stomach fluctuation of principal but need high rates of return for income may want to pay extra careful attention here: When it comes to the mentality that "I don't want to lose my principal," a lot of the time (but by no means all of the time), people worry about losing principal in the markets because if they lose money, then they are losing income. When you play the Most Dangerous Game as Dave and Donna's advisor did, then this is an unequivocal truth and a very understandable reason why so many people fear the markets. (As an important reminder, the Most Dangerous Game is when someone is relying on the speculative possibility that the value of their stocks will increase enough in value to give them the income they need. In a dividend strategy, remember: The value of the stocks is separate from the income the stocks produce.) When using the reliable returns that dividends generally provide for income, then the risk of playing the Most Dangerous Game is significantly reduced.

Here's an example that demonstrates why…

Suppose I have $100,000 to invest, and for purposes of diversifying an income-producing portfolio for possible growth and income, I like the idea of including dividend stocks as part of my investment engine. Instead of investing in individual stocks that pay dividends, I invest in closed-end funds that contain hundreds of stocks paying dividends. And instead of investing in one closed-end fund, I spread out my risk and purchase, as an example, 10 closed-end funds, investing $10,000 into each. The total dividend (or, more simply) *the income* the portfolio produces through all the closed-end funds can be as high as 7 percent or in some cases, even much higher. In dollars, and as an example, that translates into $7,000 per year being generated from this hypothetical $100,000 investment.

Now, certainly, the initial $100,000 I invested can go up or down in value. After all, I'm investing in closed-end funds that contain stocks. As such, maybe a year later the value of my initial $100,000 investment is up 10 percent, for a total value of $110,000. Maybe it falls the other way; collectively, the account is no longer worth $100,000, but went down to $80,000.

As the underlying value of my stocks within the closed-end funds goes up or down, what is the one thing that generally remains consistent? The income of $7,000, that's what. The dividends, or income, the portfolio of closed-end funds produces is in many ways more reliable than the value of the fund itself.

Why? Because remember the critical point reviewed at the beginning of this section: the *value* of the stock is *totally separate* from the *income* it produces. And as for the reliability of this income, if you have a handful of closed-end funds, and each fund likely has hundreds of individual stocks nested within it that are all working to generate income, then you can easily have a grand total of a few thousand stocks collectively paying all the dividends. A few individual stocks within the closed-end fund may very well cut their dividend or eliminating it, but with this strategy, you could have thousands of other dividend-paying stocks working to maintain the income.

Simplifying the concept of dividend stocks

Because this can get confusing, I'm going to walk you through an analogy I often use to help make the point a bit clearer.

Imagine you and I invest in real estate, purchasing a house today for $100,000 (with no mortgage). Because this is an investment, to cover our monthly expenses we rent it out to a guy named Jack. We researched Jack's track record in other properties he's rented in the past and it appears that he has never missed a payment. We have a strong belief that Jack will be a good, reliable tenant, providing us with a monthly income to cover our expenses.

Jack pays us a total annual rent (our income, otherwise known as a dividend) of, as an example, $7,000. From our original investment of $100,000, we are therefore receiving a 7 percent rate of return. If the house increases in value to $150,000, would that change our income? Not at all. We would still get our $7,000 from Jack, which continues to represent a 7 percent return on our original investment of $100,000 even though the house has gone up in value.

What if our house goes *down* in value to $80,000? Would our income being received from Jack change? Not at all. As before, we would still get our $7,000 from Jack, which continues to represent a 7 percent return on our original investment of $100,000 even though the house in this case has gone *down* in value.

So, regardless of whether the value of the house goes up, declines, or remains the same, we are still getting our $7,000 from our original investment of $100,000. This

$7,000 represents a 7 percent return, which stays the same regardless of the value of the house. Better stated, *the rent we are receiving is totally independent from the value of the house itself.* Just like a dividend-paying stock, this allows us to generate reliable cash flow from the original investment while we likely ride out the ups and downs in this case of the real estate market.

Therefore, we can safely conclude that the income (dividend) Jack pays us is totally independent from the value of the house. This same principle applies with the dividends (income) we can get from stocks. If the value goes down, Jack is still paying the rent, making the bad market years much more tolerable given the income is still there.

Now, let's take things a step further. Let's discuss some of the risk: Jack is the only guy paying us rent. He lives in the house himself. So, what's the risk here? The risk is obvious: Even though Jack has a strong history of being very reliable, maybe for whatever reason, one day Jack gets laid off from his job and stops paying the rent.

This can happen as easily with a tenant paying rent as it can with a company paying a dividend. And if it does happen, you and I are in trouble. We need that $7,000 to cover our expenses. If Jack stops paying, we aren't receiving anything. Without any backup plan in place, we might be playing the Most Dangerous Game: relying on the *speculative, possible* appreciation of our initial investment to give us the income we need; and that's not the game we ever want to be playing, because that is much more of a *market timer's game* and we are *investors*.

So, you come up with a great idea. You tell me, "Listen, instead of having *only* Jack pay the $7,000, why don't we rent the house out by the room, to *dozens* of people with great track records who *collectively* pay us an annual total of $7,000 in rental income? That way, if Jack unexpectedly falls on hard times and cuts or eliminates his rent check, we would still have many other people paying us their portion of the total income. Certainly, this would minimize the risk compared to renting only to Jack."

Therefore, *diversifying* the tenants and adding many more of them into our house makes this rental income much more reliable than if we rented the house to only Jack. This is exactly what I'm talking about when discussing the critical need to have as many dividend stocks as possible "paying you the rent." The more tenants there are paying their rent, the less likely we'll get ourselves into trouble and fall short on expenses should a few of them fail to pay. Each tenant represents a mere sliver of the engine that is producing our monthly income, thereby reducing our risk and creating a more reliable rate of return.

When you invest in dividend stocks through a portfolio of closed-end funds, there are potentially thousands of "tenants" paying you the income you count on.

Remember:

The income (dividend) a stock pays is separate from its value.

- Regardless of whether the value of the stock goes up or down, our income (dividend) generally remains the same.

- The income *might* change. Even if the company has a highly impressive track record of always paying dividends to its shareholders, there are certainly no guarantees it will always remain the same; it can even get cut entirely.

- To minimize this risk, we don't invest in only a few stocks that pay dividends; we invest in *thousands of stocks* so that if any one company reduces the dividend or eliminates it, there are many other dividend-paying stocks to help cushion such a possible fall.
- And one of the instruments we can use to diversify into dividend stocks is a closed-end fund.

The Power of Dividend Stocks

A real-world example of this concept in action will help you better understand just how powerful this can be. I'll use Dave and Donna from back in the beginning of this chapter to illustrate the point.

If you recall, at the time Dave and Donna retired, they had $2 million and needed to generate income from their nest egg that required a 7 percent needed rate of return.

Do you remember why they got into so much trouble?

They got into trouble because the advisor they were working with was dangerously *speculating* that the *value* of their stocks would grow enough to give them the income they needed. And unless you have a crystal ball all shined up and ready to go, there is no possible way of knowing if the stocks will consistently appreciate by 7 percent year after year.

So what happened?

In Dave and Donna's case, the value of the stocks didn't go up 7 percent; the value went down 15 percent. So, the 15 percent loss of value *in addition to* the 7 percent they were withdrawing for income really got them into hot water. The total loss for the year was 22 percent, making it much more difficult the following year for their portfolio to provide them with the income they needed. And if you recall, the following year, the account value went down even more while they continued drawing their income from it. What game were they playing? They were playing the Most Dangerous Game.

If at the time they needed to generate income from their portfolio the advisor had repositioned their investments so that they included dividend stocks through instruments such as closed-end funds, Dave and Donna would have likely fared much better. In the dividend-paying portfolio of stocks, as we've learned, they would have continued receiving 7 percent from the dividends without having to draw from the stocks at the same time they were going down in value.

Again, how does this happen? How could they have invested their money into a highly diversified portfolio of closed-end dividend funds paying 7 percent, then see a drop in value but still receive income of the same amount?

Because of the important point many people aren't aware of that I brought up several times before: The amount of income you receive is not based on the value of the shares, but the *quantity* of shares purchased.

So, suppose Dave and Donna invested $2 million into a well-diversified portfolio of many closed-end funds paying 7 percent dividends (this would certainly *not* be prudent, because diversification into other investments would absolutely be essential for a number of reasons. I'm using this merely to illustrate the concept).

Suppose when they invested their $2 million, that amount purchased a total of 10,000 shares. The dividends (or income) they would have received would be based on the *quantity* of these 10,000 shares, *not* the market value of them. If those shares were later worth more or less than the initial $2 million investment, it likely wouldn't matter in regards to the *income* the portfolio produces. As long as the *quantity* of shares doesn't change, when thousands of stocks inside a portfolio of closed-end funds are paying the dividends, the income generally remains the same.

This is so often overlooked, and I can't emphasize enough its importance and the value of knowing this.

Buying and Selling the Dividend Stock Portfolio

When a portfolio such as this is established, if the value of the portfolio goes down, you should generally *not* sell off any positions. Selling off shares of a closed-end fund that is producing income will reduce the number of shares in the portfolio and therefore reduce the amount of income one receives.

Selling off positions when they are down in value will recognize the loss. To understand why this can hurt you more than you may think, let's get back to Dave and Donna.

Suppose Dave and Donna's initial $2 million account was generating 7 percent for income. A year later, the value of their portfolio goes down. Let's use a very steep drop as an example. Let's say terrible things happen in the market and their overall account loses 20 percent of its value and is now worth only $1.6 million.

If Dave and Donna held the portfolio, they should generally maintain the *same* income as when they *first* invested. They continue living off their income and, while they are certainly aware of the "paper" loss, they understand they are still invested in the same *amount* of shares that could go back up in value at any time.

If they panic and sell the portfolio when it is down, in this case they would then be left with $1.6 million in cash. With the cash in hand, the next question would likely be, "Where can I now invest $1.6 million to generate the same income I need?"

Answer: most likely by having to invest in stocks for speculative growth that *could* and *might possibly* get them the return they now need. With less cash on hand, the rate of return required to produce the same amount of income they need would obviously be much higher. A higher rate of return would require riskier investments, whereby someone would very likely have little choice but to play, as we well learned before, the Most Dangerous Game.

It's for this reason an income-producing portfolio of high quality closed-end funds should generally be considered a "buy and hold" portfolio, especially if the account goes down in value. If Dave and Donna's portfolio was set up properly in the first place—in a *highly* diversified portfolio *with small amounts of money allocated to a large variety of closed-end funds*—unless there is a major problem within the portfolio, they should infrequently need to change any part of these holdings.

If the portfolio goes down in value and the income it generates is satisfying to the investor, then one would very likely want to hold the portfolio until it potentially increases back in value. Chances are you might be thinking, "What if it never comes back? What if the value stays down?"

But the *greater risk* would be the Most Dangerous Game Dave and Donna already played: In their world, when the value of the portfolio was going down, they were pulling income from the same pot of money, thereby *accelerating* the loss. Remember the bathtub analogy: They were taking water out of the tub while some of it was going down the drain at the same time.

In the case of dividends being produced through the closed-end funds, if the portfolio goes down in value, Dave and Donna would *not* be taking money from the declining value. They would be generating income from the dividends paid based on the *number of shares* that have *remained the same*. That's why it is so critical to remember that the value of the shares has little to do with the income they produce.

One of the main risks of a closed-end portfolio generating income is if dividends get cut or eliminated. It is therefore the reason why the only way anyone should ever rely on income being produced from this area of their diversified portfolio is to invest in *many* closed-end funds so that many companies are collectively paying the income, not just a few.

Furthermore, even though at the time of this writing an investor can receive dividend income as high as 10 percent (or more) from a portfolio such as this, one must not rely on this type of strategy alone. Prudent investment engines should never be constructed with one product, no matter how good it appears to be. One must always consider diversifying into bonds, stocks, CDs, and so on to prevent unforeseen problems. In this type of portfolio, if emergency cash were needed from the portfolio, it would be a disaster to pull money out of a closed-end fund if it was down in value (because, as mentioned, doing so would reduce the income). You absolutely need other areas to take money from just in case the value of this type of portfolio goes down.

Again, always ask yourself and your advisor: "What is the worst thing that can go wrong here?"

If someone cannot stomach *any* possibility that a portfolio like this can go down in value even though, presumably, the income is still being produced, then one should explore other strategies, some of which I discuss during the course of this book.

That said, there are plenty of people I have worked with over the years who need to generate high returns for income from their investments. Even though many of us would prefer to produce the income in something as completely safe as a CD, the low returns these safe instruments offer often don't provide the income we need, nor will they provide potential for growth many Baby

Boomers and retirees generally require while receiving income.

This is why educating yourself on a closed-end fund portfolio could wind up playing an important role alongside other parts of a diversified investment engine.

Ten Percent Dividends: Is That Really Possible?

When I mentioned closed-end funds that pay high dividends such 8 percent or even higher, I'm sure some of you might be thinking, "How can a stock pay that high a dividend, when most stocks pay dividends of 1 percent to as high as 6 percent?"

It would be difficult to summarize every type of closed-end fund available, but in general, the closed-end funds that pay high monthly dividends, such as ones that pay 8 percent or more, can often be categorized into a few possible areas including, but not limited to: leveraged funds and covered call funds.

Leveraged Funds. One of the advantages closed-end funds have over their close cousin, the open-ended mutual fund, is that a closed-end fund is legally allowed to use something called leverage. When you invest $1 into a closed-end fund that permits leveraging, the manager does something open-ended funds cannot do: The closed-end fund reserves the right to borrow against this $1 and invest the additional amount. For simplicity, the fund might be able to borrow 10 percent on that amount, so your $1 investment is actually purchasing roughly $1.10 of dividend-paying stocks (less the cost of the borrowed money). Add this up for the many dollars the fund collects, and you'll see that when leveraging, the fund purchases an enormous amount of additional stocks with the added borrowed money.

With more stocks purchased as a result of the borrowing, investors have more stocks working for them to produce the dividends and therefore get a higher dividend.

The danger of the leveraged funds is that their value is more volatile than that of funds that do not use leverage. The higher the leverage, the greater the dividend and the greater the risk that the value will go down. For those who don't need the higher income, I would recommend you invest in funds that do not leverage and therefore tend to be less volatile (than leveraged funds). But for those who need to count on the higher dividends for income, you may very well need to invest in leveraged funds.

Covered Calls and Covered Call Funds - A covered call is a conservative option strategy that is specifically designed to generate income. This is *not* a dividend, but some of the higher-income closed-end funds out there produce the income by doing something called "writing" covered calls against a stock index.

One covered call fund I have invested in generates an estimated income of approximately 1 percent per *month*. The underlying index the fund writes calls against is the S&P 500, and although it generates a very high income, it is still considered to be within the realm of a conservative investment. It is therefore something that could potentially be a worthy fit inside a diversified portfolio of closed-end funds.

Adding It All Up

Many investors I work with need high rates of return to generate the income they need. By "high rates of return," I'm referring to returns of 7 percent or greater. With such a need, which would you rather rely on?

Like Dave and Donna, the *possibility* that the *value* of the stocks in your portfolio will go up 7 percent year after year to provide the income you need?

Or,

Thousands of stocks within a well-diversified portfolio of closed-end mutual funds producing *dividend income* of 7 percent—income that does not rely on the speculative appreciation of stocks to generate it?

The closed-end fund is certainly not without risk, but when comparing it to playing the Most Dangerous Game, for those that don't have time to make up potential losses, it would not be hard to argue that this is the Less Dangerous Game of the two. As you dive in to explore concepts such as this for *portions* of your money, perhaps you'll feel the same way.

Final Thoughts on Closed-End Funds

When evaluating closed-end funds, be sure to check if the fund is trading at a "premium" or a "discount." These concepts are important when evaluating which fund to invest in for your diversified portfolio.

In general, when you have a choice between funds, you should typically invest in the fund that is trading at a discount rather than at a premium.

Without going into too much detail about the technical reasons and what this means, just know that when you are purchasing a fund trading at a discount, you are buying the stocks in the fund for *less* than what they are currently worth. You're buying them on sale, and that is obviously a good thing. The belief here is that because you are buying the stocks on sale, the value of the portfolio is more likely to increase (something that is certainly not guaranteed).

Conversely, purchasing closed-end funds trading at premium simply means you are paying *more* than the underlying stocks are currently worth. You are *overpaying* for the stocks. While this is not desirable, on occasion you may very well choose to invest in a closed-end fund trading at a premium as a result of the attractive income the fund produces.

In addition, closed-end funds are offered either as new issues or for purchase in the secondary market.

- A new issue is a closed-end fund that is coming out on the market and is being offered to investors for the first time. Here, the price of a new issue is fixed by the issuer.

- A secondary market closed-end fund is one that has already come out into the market. The basic laws of supply and demand establish the price of a closed-end fund offered in the secondary market.

In general, I recommend purchasing closed-end funds in the secondary market. Why? Because when you purchase new issue closed-end funds, you are going to pay loads (fees and commissions) on the issue that are built into the purchase price.

Just recently, someone asked my opinion on a closed-end fund about to be issued. On the front page of the prospectus, I showed her that the share price was $18.75, but the offering price was $20. That spread of $1.25 per share was simply the fees and commissions built into the sale of the new issue. Certainly, there are going to be times when purchasing a closed-end fund "at issue" makes much sense, so by no means take my preference as an absolute.

Ideally, an investor should first look into the secondary market before purchasing a newly issued closed-end fund. Chances are there are some quality buys out there that will cost less in fees and commissions and still satisfy the reasons for investing in a closed-end fund in the first place.

There are other factors not mentioned here to consider before investing in a closed-end fund designed to generate dividends. As with any other investment strategy discussed in this book, careful consideration should always be given before an investment is made, and it's therefore advisable to seek the assistance of a qualified advisor.

CHAPTER THREE: BONDS

As the old saying goes, "You make your money in stocks and you keep it in bonds."

When it comes to generating reliable returns, especially for income, bonds are an essential part of most diversified portfolios. As a result, I start out by addressing bonds not because they are my favorite, but because they are so often used—and for good reason.

Bonds Defined

Let's start at the very beginning by first asking, "What is a bond?" After all, if you don't really know what it is, then everything else to follow is not going to make much sense.

Simply put, a bond is a loan an investor makes to a corporation or government. In exchange for lending them money, they pay you interest on your investment, and at the end of the term, they will return the money that you gave them.

Suppose you own a business and need money. I give you $50,000 for a term of five years. And for each of those five years, you're going to pay me $3,000 (which represents a 6 percent return per year). So, at the end of the five years, I'll have accumulated $15,000 ($3,000 of interest per year for five years). In addition to keeping my $15,000 of interest, I also get my $50,000 back at the end of the five-year term—that is, at maturity. In its absolute simplest form, this is what a bond does. It provides me with a stated rate of return (in this case, 6 percent per year) for a period of time (in this case, five years).

Let's look at another example of how this could work, incorporating some additional aspects of a bond.

Suppose I am General Electric (GE) and am looking to borrow money. I offer you a bond that says: "Give me your money for five years, and for each year that I have your money, I'm going to give you 7 percent interest. At the end of five years, I'll give you your money back."

Sounds simple, right?

Okay, but what if a guy named Skip who owns a lemonade stand offers the same thing? He says, "Give me your money for five years, and for each year I have your money, I'm going to give you the same interest—7 percent. And, at the end of five years, I'll give you your money back as well."

What would your first concern be?

Most likely, something such as, "How do I know some guy named Skip won't skip out on me with my money? How do I know he will still be in business in five years?" In this case, wouldn't it make much more sense to lend a company such as GE your money, given it has been around for a very long time and as a result you know it'll still be around in five years?

Knowing this, Skip, who is a sharp guy, comes back to you and ups the ante: For each year he has your money, he's going to give you *15 percent* interest, and at the end of five years, he'll give you your money back. At that rate of return, you might be tempted to give Skip some of your money. True, there is more risk, but now you're being paid more for the higher risk and it's somewhat enticing.

What we're talking about here is another component of a bond, its credit quality. In general, the *lower* the credit quality, the *higher* the interest. In addition, the *longer* the period of time someone is borrowing your money, the *higher* the interest rate typically is. After all, if they are keeping your money for a longer period of time, then there is an increased chance more things can go wrong, and you should be rewarded for that risk, which is typically the case.

Among other factors to consider when investing in a bond, another important thing you should know about bonds is how marketable, or *liquid* your investment would be. Would anyone else be willing to take over that bond if I needed to sell it? Perhaps you lent GE money for those five years, but let's say two years in, for whatever reason, suppose you wanted to get your money out of the investment by selling it to someone else.

To get your money out, you would need to offer that GE bond into something called the secondary market, the area of the investment universe where others presumably seek what you have and make offers on it. In the secondary market, however, you might not get back the same amount you first invested. If you held it for the five years (to the bond's maturity date), unless GE had significant problems, you would get your money back, but here you are looking to sell it early, which means that you could get back more *or* less than you invested.

Here's why:

The Seesaw Effect of Bonds

Suppose you buy that GE bond for $10,000 and it has an interest rate of 7 percent. A little while later, you want to sell that bond to someone else. However, people can now buy new bonds of the same credit quality and maturity date that pay 10 percent interest, not 7 percent.

Who would want to buy your bond paying 7 percent? No one unless the math was adjusted.

The only way someone would want to buy that bond is if they can get a *comparable* return of 10 percent. So, how would they make it comparable to 10 percent? Simple: They will give you less money for that bond so that their return is essentially the same as if they were buying a new bond offering 10 percent.

The same thing works in reverse. Suppose you wanted to sell that bond paying 7 percent, but at that time the same type of bonds are paying only 4 percent. The only way it would make sense for you to sell that bond is if someone paid you *more* than what you had invested.

If it sounds a bit confusing, think of this little visual I learned while in elementary school. While it doesn't solve the math, it'll help you understand what's known as the "inverse" relationship between the values and interest rates of bonds. It has stayed in my mind since somewhere around the fifth grade and maybe it'll help you as well.

If you've ever been to a playground, you most likely know what a seesaw is. Two kids sit facing each other on opposite ends of a long board. Between them is a block supporting the board off the ground. As one kid goes up, the other goes down.

One kid is named "Interest Rate" and the other is "Value." As one goes up, the other goes down, and vice versa. If the Interest Rate kid goes up, Value goes down.

The same thing happens in reverse: If Interest Rate goes down, Value goes up.

"One thing going up while the other thing goes down" is known as the inverse relationship between bond value and interest rates: They move in opposite directions from each other.

Taking it one step further, the *length* of that seesaw is also important. The length—or in terms of bonds, the maturity date (how many years you have to hold that bond before you get your money back)—is also deserving of a visual: The longer the seesaw, the more the value will typically be affected.

You will frequently hear bonds classified as short-term, intermediate-term, and long-term. A quick explanation of each should help you gain a better understanding of the pros and cons, as well as the way that the length of the term affects the value.

- *Short-term bonds (less than five years to maturity).* Building on the seesaw example, assume that the two kids are sitting very, very close to each other on opposite ends of the short board. When the Interest Rate kid goes up, the Value kid goes down. However, because they are sitting so close to each other, there isn't much of a change in their movement. This visual demonstrates the trends seen in short-term bonds, which typically do not fluctuate much in value. Because short-term bonds have less fluctuation in value, they are generally assumed to be *safer* than longer-term bonds.

- *Long-term bonds (over 10 years to maturity).* Now imagine a very, very long seesaw. This one is called a long-term bond. As the Interest Rate kid rises, Value on the other end drops. In long-term bonds, the fluctuation in value can be quite dramatic, and they are therefore assumed to be riskier. If you want to get your money out before the maturity date, then there is a more significant chance the value could be far more or less than the amount you initially invested.

- *Intermediate-term bonds (5 to 10 years to maturity).* Intermediate bonds, as their name suggests, fall between the short- and long-term bonds.

Bottom line: The longer the seesaw (maturity date), the more the value of the bond can fluctuate. Logically, then, in case someone had to sell a bond prior to the maturity date, wouldn't most people prefer to stay in short-term bonds? Not always. In general, the longer the maturity date, the higher the interest rate is on the bond. While that is not always the case, it is typical and therefore the reason people often invest some of their money in longer-term bonds to get the higher reliable return they desire. (More on this coming soon.)

Now that you understand a bit more about bonds and the way they operate, let's take a closer look at how to invest in them so that you can generate some reliable rates of return for your diversified portfolio.

Individual Bonds versus Bond Mutual Funds

When investing in bonds to produce a reliable return, one can invest in an individual bond or, commonly, a diversified pool of bonds. For many people, investing in a diversified pool of bonds is often done by investing into a bond *mutual fund*.

In general, I advise people, especially those in retirement, to stay away from investing in bond mutual funds as much as possible. Only if someone has a small amount of money to invest ($50,000 or less) should they consider using a bond mutual fund.

However, bond funds are a mainstay for many investors seeking reliable income and the stability of a diversified investment portfolio, and with understandable reason. Because a bond fund is a group of bonds chosen and managed by a money manager, it provides professional management and quick diversification among a large number of different bonds. This could help cushion a portfolio from one of the bonds defaulting (not paying interest or going bankrupt), which brings us to another important point about bonds.

Whereas investing in bonds is generally safer than investing in stocks, they are certainly not without risk. Aside from the possibility that a company may go out of business, when interest rates rise the value of the bonds will likely fall, as will the value of the bond mutual fund as a whole.

Unlike an individual bond, a bond mutual fund does not have a maturity date—the wonderful date every investor looks forward to, when you know the money you invested is going to be returned to you. This is obviously a very attractive feature of an individual bond that a bond mutual fund doesn't offer.

If the value of an individual bond goes down, you know the date (maturity) when you are getting your money back.

Conversely, if the value of a bond mutual fund goes down, you do *not* know when you will get your money back, because there is no maturity date. You don't know when the value of the bond fund might return to its initial value, if at all. It is for this reason I generally recommend individual bonds when investing to achieve reliable rates of return with as little risk as possible.

But as with all investment strategies, there are advantages and disadvantages. I wish it were simpler; it would save us all a bit of time and paper, but unfortunately, when it comes to investing, things are never quite as black-and-white as we'd like. No doubt, this is where having to choose between a bond and a bond mutual fund can get somewhat confusing. Thankfully, however, when it comes to bonds, I do believe there is an answer that satisfies the advantages and disadvantages of both. More on this coming up.

On the one hand, investing in an individual bond means there is a date (the maturity date) when you are due to get your money back. That's great, but when investing in an individual bond, there is certainly risk that the company you lent your money to could go out of business.

On the other hand, if you invest in a bond mutual fund, you have many bonds working for you. If one company defaults (goes out of business), it won't have a dramatic effect on your overall investment because there are many other bonds in the mix to buffer one evil bond's demise.

So, the *diversification* of having many bonds in a fund certainly decreases the risk; if one hair on the head is lost, there are many others on the head to still keep things looking pretty. But here's where the paradox comes in: The disadvantage to the bond fund, as mentioned before, is that if interest rates rise and the value of the fund goes down, you have no idea when your investment will "come back." Certainly, many advisors will tell you to diversify and to hold on until it does come back, but remember: We are not market timers or gamblers. We are investors, and every single step of the way, as much as possible, we are always looking to give ourselves the best chances for success while asking ourselves the constant questions, "What's the worst thing that can go wrong with this portfolio?"

With that, when it comes to wanting the diversification of a bond fund *and* the maturity date that an individual bond offers, in this case there is a way to have your cake and eat it, too.

Before I reveal the timeless answer, it is important that you understand where the risks and rewards are when choosing between an individual bond and a bond mutual fund. To help summarize the advantages and disadvantages, the table below offers a quick summary of a few important differences between an individual bond and a bond mutual fund.

Bond Funds vs Bond Ladders

	BOND FUND	BOND LADDER
Maturity Date (is there a *date* when investors know they will likely get their investment back?)	No	Yes
Risk	Less than an individual bond due to increased diversification	More than a bond fund due to less diversification
Income	Can be the same	

As you can see, the attractive features one has that the other does not make choosing between the two a bit difficult. So, is there a way to get the best of *both* worlds? To take the good of both and as much as possible eliminate the bad?

There sure is, and the answer is one of my favorite reliable return investment strategies, designed to preserve your money *and* create a reliable return that is independent from stocks. The answer is: Create your own bond mutual fund, otherwise known as a bond ladder.

Bond Ladders

Bond ladders provide the advantages of both individual bonds and bond mutual funds. We'll soon find out why. The main disadvantage of bond ladders is that they are not as simple to invest in as, in comparison, a bond fund generally is.

But, I firmly believe the rewards of investing in a bond ladder far outweigh the additional time it takes to create one. No doubt, if you have never created a bond ladder for yourself, this is definitely one area of your investment portfolio that you'll want to get some assistance on. And by reading this section, you'll have a great head start in working with your advisor in creating one. And who knows? Maybe you'll even teach the advisor a thing or two, given that many advisors rarely use it, perhaps because of the additional time it takes to create one or, perhaps, the higher fees earned on many mutual funds.

Suppose I have $100,000 to invest, and let's also suppose that I need to generate some reliable returns from this money. In case the stock indexes in my diversified portfolio go down in value, I want a hedge to ensure that at least one part of my portfolio is delivering reliable returns for my income needs.

There could be many reasons why I would invest in a bond ladder, but the bottom line is this: At this moment in time, for whatever reason, suppose I need to get myself a 6 percent rate of return, or in dollars, $6,000 off my $100,000 investment.

After reading and understanding the differences between various investment vehicles we have discussed to this point, I don't want to play the Most Dangerous Game by counting on stock appreciation to try to give me that return. I want to invest that $100,000 in something secure and reliable that will deliver the $6,000 I need without the speculation that it *might* happen in the stock markets.

So, after investigating various possible choices, I like the idea of bonds. I venture out into the marketplace and feel really lucky when I find that GE, a very solid company with great credit quality, has a bond that will pay me 6 percent. With this reliable return meeting my investment requirements, I figure, "I'll take it. Why invest anywhere else?"

Comfortable in my decision, through the bond, I lend GE my $100,000 and all is fine. I'm happy with my 6 percent return per year and it seems that I've made the right choice. But then the bond matures (I get my money back at the end of the term), or it gets called. ("Called" simply means GE has the right to return my money at any time before the maturity date. This is a common feature of many bonds, and typically when a bond is called it's not a good thing, for reasons I'm about to explain.)

I get my money back, and have to start searching the bond market for another bond. I like the idea that the GE bond offers safety of principal (at maturity when you get your money back) and that I am provided with the "bird in the hand" reliable return of 6 percent.

While it's nice that I got my money back (at maturity or when GE called it), in this hypothetical example, I am disappointed to learn GE bonds and others like it are not paying 6 percent any longer; they are only paying, as an example, 4 percent.

That's not good. I need 6 percent to satisfy my reliable return requirements and there are no good credit quality bonds available in the marketplace that can provide me with this return. The risk of this happening is what's known as interest rate risk or reinvestment risk, and it's a risk that investors who rely on bonds may run into from time to time; when a bond matures or gets called and you get your money back, you may not find another bond with an equal rate of return, years to maturity, and quality.

To give you the best possible chance to avoid these risks, a bond ladder does the following:

- Minimizes interest rate and reinvestment risk.
- Diversifies your bond portfolio.
- Includes many maturity dates, the dates where you typically get back your original investment.

- Maintains a reliable and predictable rate of return to help hedge the possibility that the stock portion of the portfolio may go down in value.

A bond ladder is simply a portfolio of individual bonds with staggered (different) maturity dates. Think of a bond ladder as your very own bond mutual fund, without the management fees and *with* maturity dates (the date at which you know your money is being returned to you). This is a highly efficient strategy that many advisors and investors often overlook. I find the reason it is often overlooked is because setting up a bond ladder requires more work than investing in a mutual fund does. But is it worth the extra time? In most cases, I absolutely think so.

Suppose you have $100,000 to invest in your own bond ladder. You don't have one bond paying you 6 percent, but you might have 10 bonds with a value of $10,000 each. In a well-structured bond ladder, the bonds would have varying maturities, with one bond maturing in a year, another in two years, another in three years, and so forth. The resulting portfolio would look like a ladder, as you will see shortly in my example. Most important, the *entire ladder,* not just one bond, pays you an aggregate total of 6 percent (needless to say, this 6 percent is just an example—rates can be higher or lower depending on many different factors and economic conditions).

The main benefit of this investment strategy is that by laddering, or staggering, the maturity dates of the bonds, you won't be locked into any particular bond for any significant length of time, which gives you much greater flexibility on a number of levels.

Let's say that you invest your $100,000 in that single GE bond with a 6 percent yield and a 10-year maturity. During the 10 years that you're going to hold that bond, interest rates are likely to rise and fall and the bond value will follow suit.

As mentioned, if interest rates are low at the time your bond matures—and you're ready to invest in another bond—you'll be stuck buying a bond with a low interest rate. Not good.

However, if you have constructed a bond ladder, only *one* of the many bonds in your portfolio will mature at any given time. So although interest rates may be low when one bond matures, chances are the interest rate environment will be different when the other bonds mature, thereby giving you a much better chance of sustaining the rate of return that made you comfortable to invest in the bond ladder in the first place.

Bond laddering is particularly beneficial in a rising interest rate environment because it allows you to readily move your money out of lower-yielding bonds and into those with higher yields as interest rates rise. One could argue that if you buy shares of a bond fund, the portfolio manager would do this for you, but again, just remember that bond mutual funds have no maturity dates. If the value of the fund drops, you have no idea when your investment is going to be returned to you, if ever.

Remember that important consideration I mentioned before: Investors looking at their portfolios should always be asking themselves the question, "What is the worst thing that can happen here?"

In a portfolio of bond mutual funds, the worst thing that can happen is that interest rates can rise, causing the values of the funds to go down, and if investors need to remove money from this area, they will be getting back less than the amount invested. Or, if the value of the funds goes down and investors need more income, then they have to sell at a loss and possibly reinvest the smaller amount somewhere else to try to give themselves a higher return.

Those are certainly not the best options. These are scenarios that should be considered when asking, "What's the worst thing that can happen here?" And it's the reason that, as much as possible, I tend to shy away from bond mutual funds that cannot assure an investor that if the fund loses value, they will get their money back. I'd much prefer the reduced risk that comes with a well-diversified portfolio of quality, laddered individual bonds.

Bond Ladders Offer Flexibility of Interest Rates

A secondary benefit of bond laddering is that it lets you or your advisor adjust the interest you receive from the bonds. With a single bond, what you see is what you get. With bond laddering, you have plenty of room to tweak your portfolio to generate results that work best for you.

Suppose your bond ladder provides you with a combined return of 6 percent, but for whatever reason, you need an extra percentage point, 7 percent. To get that extra percentage point, you can usually swap one bond on the ladder for another. Typically, to get that extra yield you would either increase the maturity length of a bond or invest in a bond of a lesser credit quality.

Incorporating one of these elements, or a combination of the two, will usually get you that extra yield. Needless to say, adjusting maturity dates and credit quality can bring additional risk into the ladder. Therefore, you never want to overload an investment into one bond, but rather spread the risk out among many bonds.

Let's take a look at an example:

Suppose you are investing in bonds and want or need to generate that reliable return of $6,000 per year. You have $100,000 to invest. You can certainly put the full $100,000 into that one GE bond paying 6 percent. But that puts all your eggs in one basket, and furthermore it won't provide you with the flexibility you'd have from laddering the $100,000 into several bonds, as shown below.

Sample Bond Ladder

BOND	AMOUNT	YIELD	INCOME
1	10,000	4.0%	$400
2	10,000	4.5%	$450
3	10,000	5.0%	$500
4	10,000	5.5%	$550
5	10,000	6.0%	$600
6	10,000	6.0%	$600

7	10,000	7.0%	$700
8	10,000	7.0%	$700
9	10,000	7.0%	$700
10	10,000	8.0%	$800
	Return:	6.0%	$6,000

You're still getting your 6 percent for income, but you are not painting yourself into a corner with just one bond. As the years roll on and bonds in the ladder mature one after the other, you would be continually rolling into a new bond to maintain the reliable return requirements. Even as I write this in a relatively low interest rate environment, maturing bonds are being reallocated into other bonds that are maintaining the reliable return requirements.

Am I Locked into a Bond Ladder?

The entire bond ladder is liquid and can be sold off at any time. Just know that while you own the bonds, the yield won't change but the *value* of the bonds could. Depending on what happens with interest rates during the bond ladder period, the *value* of each bond can rise or fall. As bond values rise and fall, there are many opportunities for adjusting the ladder.

For instance, yield and length of maturity can be updated by selling the bond and replacing it with another one. However, selling a bond prior to its maturity date would make sense only if you can invest in a different bond that will provide you with higher yield, while decreasing the length of time until maturity and/or purchasing a bond of equal or higher credit quality.

The locked-in maturity date typically comes into effect only if the bond decreases in value and you want to know when your original investment will be returned to you. The answer, of course, is at maturity when the bond reaches its full face value. Remember, however, that if you sell the bond prior to maturity, you will get whatever value the secondary market places on the bond at the time you sell it.

In summary, bond ladders provide comfort in knowing:

- With good credit quality bonds (investment grade), your investment is generally quite safe, especially when compared to stocks.
- Bond ladders provide a predetermined, reliable, and predictable rate of return, which is helpful toward

generating income or hedges against the stock portion of your diversified portfolio if it goes down in value.

- Finally, bond ladders provide flexibility in being able to adjust the ladder when interest rates change.

Before moving to the next area of creating reliable returns, there are a few other things you should know about bonds.

Duration

For instant diversification, ease of investing, or any other reason, you might very well wind up investing in a bond fund. As mentioned, I usually stay away from them, but many people do use them and find that they suit their needs.

For those of you who invest in bond mutual funds, you should at least be aware of two key figures provided by the fund: average maturity and average duration.

Average maturity is the average time period until the bonds in a fund mature, and this period is usually quoted in years. Why look at this number? Generally speaking, bond funds with lower average maturities experience less fluctuation to their value than bond funds with higher average maturities (assuming that both types of funds have comparable credit quality). As a result, bond funds with lower average maturities typically have less interest rate risk.

Average duration is an even better reflection of a bond fund's sensitivity to interest rate changes. Duration indicates the change in the value of a bond fund for each 1 percent change in interest rates. For example, let's say the bonds in Fund A have an average duration of three years. That means that for each 1 percent change in interest rates, the bond fund's value (or price) should move 3 percent (1 percent × 3 years) in the opposite direction of the interest rate change. So in this example, if interest rates rise 1 percent, Fund A's value should fall 3 percent.

Another example: Let's say the bonds in Fund B have an average duration of 10 years. For each 1 percent change in interest rates, the bond fund's price should move 10 percent—again, in the opposite direction of the interest rate change. When interest rates rise 1 percent, the bond fund's price should fall 10 percent.

As the examples illustrate, the lower the average duration of the bonds held in a fund, the less the bond fund's value should fall when interest rates rise. These calculations can get complicated, but most portfolio managers do the work for you by classifying their bond funds according to average duration. Short-term funds, for instance, generally hold bonds that mature within one to four years. Intermediate-term funds generally hold bonds maturing in five to 10 years. And long-term funds generally hold bonds that mature in 10 years or more.

The lesson: If you want to stay in bond funds and minimize the risk as much as possible, find a fund that is classified as short-term, or funds that have short duration. Morningstar's web site (www.morningstar.com) is a good resource to help evaluate the duration of your funds, or funds your advisor might be considering for your money.

Do you understand the concept of duration? I hope so, because if you are going to invest in a bond fund, it's certainly useful to have a grasp of duration, especially since I find some advisors don't always take into consideration the duration of the fund.

Credit Qualities

Lastly, we've learned that it's important to pay attention to the credit quality of the bonds in your ladder or your mutual fund. The two agencies that are most frequently referred to in assigning ratings to corporate bond issuers are Moody's Investors Service (Moody's) and Standard & Poor's Corporation (S&P). Both firms focus on a company's financial condition and the state of the industry in which it operates at that particular point in time. The agencies often revise their ratings of companies, so it's important to make sure you are looking at current ratings and not the ratings from years ago.

Conceptually, corporate bonds are broken down into two categories: investment grade and below investment grade (aka junk bonds, which, for marketing purposes, the companies have conveniently renamed high-yield bonds).

Investment grade bonds carry less risk than junk bonds. As a rule of thumb, if you see a bond in your ladder paying an abnormally high rate of interest, chances are great that it is a junk bond issued by a company that has a poor credit rating.

The table below summarizes the different ratings that Moody's and S&P place on bonds.

INVESTMENT GRADE

Highest Grades

Moody's	**Aaa**	Best quality, smallest degree of risk.
S&P	**AAA**	Ability to meet financial obligation on the bond is extremely strong.

High Grades

Moody's	**Aa1, Aa2, Aa3**	High quality by all standards. Not as strong as highest grade.
S&P	**AA+, AA, AA–**	Ability to meet financial obligation on the bond is very strong.

Upper Medium Grades

Moody's	**A1, A2, A3**	Many favorable investment attributes, secure.
S&P	**A+, A, A–**	The issuer's capacity to meet its financial obligations is strong.

Medium Grades

Moody's	**Baa1, Baa2, Baa3**	Speculative characteristics.
S&P	**BBB+, BBB, BBB–**	Adverse conditions are likely to lead to speculative possibilities about whether the issuer will meet its obligations.

BELOW INVESTMENT GRADE

Speculative Grades

Moody's	**Ba1, Ba2,**	The future of these

	Ba3; B1, B2, B3	bonds cannot be considered as stable.
S&P	BB+, BB, BB–; B+, B, B–	These bonds face exposure to adverse business or economic conditions that could lead to an issuer's inadequate capacity to meet its financial commitment.

Highly Speculative Grades

Moody's	Caa1, Caa2, Caa3; Ca	These bonds are of poor standing. Such issuers may be in default, or in significant danger of not meeting obligations.
S&P	CCC+, CCC, CCC–; CC, C	These bonds are vulnerable to nonpayment, and are dependent upon favorable economic conditions for the issuer to meet its financial commitment.

Default

Moody's	C	These bonds are typically in default, with little prospect for recovery of principal or interest.
S&P	D	These bonds are in payment default.

INVESTMENT GRADE

Highest Grades

Moody's	**Aaa**	Best quality, smallest degree of risk.
S&P	**AAA**	Ability to meet financial obligation on the bond is extremely strong.

High Grades

Moody's	**Aa1, Aa2, Aa3**	High quality by all standards. Not as strong as highest grade.
S&P	**AA+, AA, AA–**	Ability to meet financial obligation on the bond is very strong.

Upper Medium Grades

Moody's	**A1, A2, A3**	Many favorable investment attributes, secure.
S&P	**A+, A, A–**	The issuer's capacity to meet its financial obligations is strong.

Medium Grades

Moody's	**Baa1, Baa2, Baa3**	Speculative characteristics.
S&P	**BBB+, BBB, BBB–**	Adverse conditions are likely to lead to speculative possibilities about whether the issuer will meet its obligations.

BELOW INVESTMENT GRADE

Speculative Grades

Moody's	**Ba1, Ba2, Ba3; B1, B2, B3**	The future of these bonds cannot be considered as stable.
S&P	**BB+, BB, BB–; B+, B, B–**	These bonds face exposure to adverse business or economic conditions that could lead to an issuer's inadequate capacity to meet its financial commitment.

Highly Speculative Grades

Moody's	**Caa1, Caa2, Caa3; Ca**	These bonds are of poor standing. Such issuers may be in default, or in significant danger of not meeting obligations.
S&P	**CCC+, CCC, CCC–; CC, C**	These bonds are vulnerable to nonpayment, and are dependent upon favorable economic conditions for the issuer to meet its financial commitment.

Default

Moody's	C	These bonds are typically in default, with little prospect
		for recovery of principal or interest.
S&P	**D**	These bonds are in payment default.

Taxes

My previous examples have not included a discussion on taxes. As with any discussion on taxes, given there are so many considerations to take into account based on someone's personal situation, please make sure you discuss your intentions with a qualified tax or investment advisor before taking action.

In general:

- Interest from corporate bonds is fully taxable as ordinary income, which, as we'll find out later on, is the least favorable type of tax.
- Interest from government bonds is generally taxed as ordinary income at the federal level only.
- Interest from municipal bonds is generally tax-free both at the federal level and state level (as long as you reside in the state where the bond was issued or you live in an income tax free state such as Florida).

When constructing a bond ladder portfolio (or any investment portfolio, for that matter), it is important to consider the actual after-tax return when evaluating the income the ladder produces. On occasion, it will make sense to use municipal bonds within the ladder, given that the interest from these bonds is often tax-free. That said, some people rush a bit too fast into municipal bonds simply because they hear those kind words "tax-free." But tax-free isn't always the best way to go.

Let's take a brief look.

Municipal Bonds

"Munis," as municipal bonds are frequently called, are one of the safest investments around, especially if they are AAA-rated and/or insured. Just a tiny fraction of municipal government bonds issued have ever defaulted. The best thing about munis, though, is that the interest they generate is typically tax-free.

Depending on your tax bracket, short-term munis or laddering longer-term munis with different maturity dates could give you attractive reliable returns while still providing a high level of safety. Up until the maturity date, just like corporate bonds, values on munis will fluctuate as well. But thanks to maturity dates, you can be assured that you'll get your money back.

To determine whether a muni bond's tax-free interest provides a higher rate of return than a taxable corporate or government bond, use the following formula (apologies – I've tried refraining from complicated formulas in this book but to do it right, there's no easy way around this one):

Tax-free yield/(1 – Your federal tax bracket)

As an example, suppose the yield on a taxable corporate bond is 5 percent, while the yield on a tax-free bond is 3 percent and your federal tax bracket is 28 percent. With this information, you would then take the tax-free yield of 3 percent and divide it by 0.72 (1 – 0.28 = 0.72), giving you an after-tax equivalent yield of 4.1 percent. In this case, the taxable corporate bond yielding 5 percent is higher than the tax-free equivalent muni yield of 4.1 percent, making the corporate bond a better choice. Although the interest from the corporate bond is taxable, the *after-tax* amount is still higher than the *tax-free* muni, making the corporate bond a better choice.

Your tax bracket and the comparison between the taxable and tax-free yields will help determine which bond would provide better results.

More Recent Developments: 8% tax free?

One of the most exciting developments for generating investment income is tax-free closed end exchange traded bond funds (**CEETBFs**). These investments are similar to muni bond mutual funds in that they contain a portfolio of different municipal bonds and thus offer instant diversification. However, tax-free CEETBFs usually have much lower fees and lower expenses than those charged by muni bond mutual funds. For example, they usually do not charge front-end loads, back-end loads or 12(b)1 fees. In addition, the annual management fees of CEETBFs tend to be much lower than the annual fees of many muni bond mutual funds.

An example clarifies the differences between muni bond mutual funds and CEETBFs. If you spent $100,000 to purchase an A share muni bond fund, you might pay a 4.75% up front fee. Additional fees charged by the fund, such as 12(b)1 fees, management fees, etc. might add up to another 1%. If the muni bond mutual fund paid 5% per year, you would actually lose money the first year you owned it.

If you instead invested $100,000 in a tax-free CEETBF, your transaction cost might only be $30 or so if you use a fee-only financial advisor. To assemble and manage a portfolio of tax-free CEETBFs, the advisor might charge a 1% annual fee. On a tax-free $100,000 CEETBF portfolio paying 5% per year, you would thus make about $4,000 per year in tax-free interest. This puts you more than $5,000 ahead of the person who bought the A share muni bond mutual fund.

The yields from tax-free CEETBFs also far surpass the after-tax return of CDs and money market accounts. In fact, it might take a CD two years to earn as much after-tax income as you can earn in one year with a carefully selected tax-free CEETBF.

Some financial advisors charge commissions instead of fees. You might pay several hundred dollars to purchase each CEETBF position in your portfolio and to sell it. Overall, commissions may add up to less than annual fees, and building a tax-free CEETBF portfolio on a commission basis could save you money.

Other Benefits of Tax-Free CEETBFs

In addition to offering instant diversification, low fees and low expenses, tax-free CEETBFs do not suffer from stale pricing. Most muni bond mutual funds are priced only once a day. Thus, the price of a mutual fund during the day is stale or old. All investors get the price of the fund on that day.

Most CEETBFs are priced continuously throughout the day. What this means is that you will *always* get the best available price. Your financial advisor can also put in a limit order to buy the CEETBF *below* the current asking price.

If the specified *lower* price is reached during the day and if your order is filled, you could save several hundred to more than one thousand dollars. Mutual funds do not offer this moment-by-moment pricing and the benefits it offers.

Another advantage of many tax-free CEETBFs is *liquidity*. You might be reluctant to sell a B share mutual fund because you could face charges of several thousand dollars on a $100,000 investment. These high exit fees on B-share mutual funds act as a surrender charge or early withdrawal fee and limit liquidity.

However, you don't have to worry about such back-end charges on tax-free CEETBFs. There are no such fees on closed end exchange traded muni bond funds. You are free to sell your CEETBFs at any time—without paying a penalty.

In my work as an income specialist, I have found that some tax-free CEETBFs offer rates of return that no muni bond mutual fund can match. For example, in some states, you can now receive more than **8% tax-free each year**. As far as I know, no muni bond mutual fund offers returns this high.

You might think that to get returns this high you have to compromise the quality of the bonds in the CEETBF. In fact, with careful research it is possible to find CEETBFs paying more than 6% tax-free that are nearly **100% invested in AAA rated municipal bonds**. Furthermore, some CEETBFs offer a bond portfolio that is nearly **100% insured**. It may seem impossible to find a 6% tax-free, AAA rated investment that also offers insurance protection, but certain tax-free CEETBFs do indeed offer this one of a kind combination of benefits.

Challenges in Building a Tax-Free CEETBF Portfolio

The many unique advantages of tax-free CEETBFs have led some people to call them "the perfect investment." They are not. All investments have risk and tax-free CEETBFs are no exception.

Some muni bonds and muni bond funds are subject to alternative minimum tax (AMT). Some tax-free CEETBFs are also subject to AMT. If you do not know how to evaluate this, you need to work with an income specialist who can help you find investments with minimal or no exposure to AMT.

Do not be afraid to pay some AMT. It may make sense to buy certain CEETBFs that are subject to a small amount of AMT in return for a much higher yield. For example, one tax-free fund might pay 5.8% per year and be subject to a 5% AMT tax. Another tax-free fund might pay 5% per year and have no AMT exposure. You would be far ahead by buying the first fund. After paying the 5% tax, your net yield would be 5.51% tax free which is still much higher than the 5% yield offered by the second fund.

Evaluating NAV and State Taxes

Tax-free CEETBFs sell below, at or above net asset value (NAV). *Net asset value* refers to the total value of the muni bonds held by the fund. With all other things being equal, it is better to buy a fund that is selling *below* net asset value. Buying at 5% below NAV is like buying $100 worth of assets for only $95. An income specialist can help you find tax-free CEETBFs selling below NAV.

The only time you want to buy a fund selling above NAV is if it is of exceptionally high quality, offers a high yield and if there are no other viable alternatives.

Some CEETBFs are subject to state taxes. Unless you live in a state with no state taxes, if you buy an out-of-state fund you will avoid federal tax but will probably have to pay state tax. Why would you ever want to buy an out-of-state fund? Out of state funds can sometimes offer higher yields.

The funds of some states pay significantly higher dividends than those of other states. For example, your portfolio of in-state CEETBFs might yield $35,000 in tax-free income per year. However, a portfolio of out-of-state funds might pay you $42,000. Even after paying your state taxes (you will never owe federal taxes on either portfolio), you might come out ahead with out-of-state funds. A skilled financial advisor specializing in income investments can help you make investments that *maximize* your after-tax returns.

Building Your Tax-Free Income Portfolio

Tax-free exchange traded funds closed end muni bond funds are generating tremendous excitement among income specialists yet are still relatively unknown to many financial advisors. Few books have yet been published on these innovative new investments.

Not all tax-free funds are superior investments. Some offer returns as low as 2% per year. Some have excessive fees. Some are subject to a high alternative minimum tax. Some contain risky bonds. Some contain many bonds that are not insured.

It is challenging and difficult work to evaluate and assemble a portfolio of high-quality tax-free funds that pay a good rate of interest. However, **the rewards are well worth the effort**. Imagine being able to earn 5% to 8% per year tax-free, without having to worry about the ups and downs of the stock market. Imagine being able to

double the after-tax returns of CDs. Imagine being able to earn five years of money market interest in one year, and *pay no taxes on it.*

CHAPTER FOUR: CERTIFICATES OF DEPOSITS

When 6 Percent = 0 Percent

Investing for reliable returns can take many shapes and forms. Another investment people can consider for the slice of their portfolio they want to keep safe and earn a reliable return on is, of course, a certificate of deposit (CD).

When striving for reliable rates of return on your investments, CDs are an obvious choice. While many investment portfolios are quite deserving of having one or many CDs within their presence, surprisingly, a CD isn't always a riskless investment.

To illustrate, consider the following question: "How is it possible to earn a 6 percent return on an investment but actually wind up making 0 percent?" When it comes to investing in CDs, it may be a bit easier than you might think.

Sheila is a friend of mine from Southern California. Years ago, Sheila got divorced and ended up with a few hundred thousand dollars. Having little experience in the stock markets, she recruited an advisor, who invested her money in various individual stocks. Within a year or two, although the advisor was doing a pretty good job diversifying the account, the markets got the best of many investors and Sheila's account wound up losing a moderate amount of money. Having a very low tolerance for risk, Sheila panicked and pulled all of her money out of the market, placed it in CDs, and vowed to never invest in anything but CDs ever again.

For safety of principal, there's no doubt that CDs offer peace of mind. But is a CD really safe? When it comes to Sheila's situation, not exactly. In fact, it can easily be argued that she's actually *losing* money in her CDs every year.

By the time Sheila caught up to me, at that time, most of her CDs were paying right around 6 percent. For simplicity, for every $100,000 invested, she was earning her $6,000 per year. That sounds like a decent return, but hold on a second. It's not as great as you may think. Sheila saw the guaranteed rate of return, but did not see the whole picture.

First of all, that $6,000 is going to show up on page 1 of her tax return as income that will be reported on Schedule B in the Part I section entitled "Interest." Sheila was in the 28 percent tax bracket. So, in the 28 percent tax bracket, Sheila will pay over a thousand dollars in tax on the $6,000, reducing her real return to just over $4,000. All of a sudden, her 6 percent CD is now really paying her approximately 4 percent. But it's not over yet.

Next up is what many commonly refer to as the "hidden tax"—the one we all pay, otherwise known as inflation. Depending on the source you listen to, inflation typically runs at around 3 percent. Many say it's considerably higher, but the government doesn't want to agree. Why? Well, many of the government entitlement programs are pegged to the inflation rate. If inflation is reported too high, then guess what happens? Uncle Sam has to raise the amount it pays to all people in various entitlement programs. Can the government afford to raise the income for these programs? Not quite. Not only is the federal deficit high enough as it is and only getting worse, but there are significant problems within the under funded Social Security system itself. Having to pay out more money due to higher reported inflation would only make things worse.

Let's get back to Sheila's CD. So far, we have learned that, no thanks to taxes owed on her CD interest, she may have *believed* she was earning 6 percent, but in reality, because she pays tax on that interest, she's really earning just over 4 percent. Factoring in inflation, which I will moderately assume runs at 3 percent, Sheila's real rate of return on that CD is actually not much more than 1 percent.

As if that's not bad enough, the situation for those in retirement could be even worse. For those in retirement collecting Social Security benefits, the interest generated from CDs could easily cause the investor to pay more taxes on their Social Security benefits.

When factoring in the additional tax one could be paying on Social Security as a result of interest being earned on a CD, it's sad, but true: The actual return on a CD paying 6 percent can easily be 0 percent, meaning a certificate of deposit can sometimes be more appropriately deemed a "certificate of *depreciation*."

Am I saying that one shouldn't invest in CDs? Not at all, in fact, I would venture to say *more* people should be investing in them (as I discussed earlier with investors such as Stock Market Stan who I believed had far too much money in the stock markets). I can think of plenty of reasons why someone should consider having CDs in their portfolio, including:

- *Diversification.* As much as the argument could hold true that 6 percent can actually equal 0 percent, there are situations that still make investing some money in CDs a perfectly prudent investment. For example, I can think of several clients of mine who have quite a bit of money in stocks, real estate, and so on, and for them, having some money in CDs is most certainly not a bad choice.

- *An elderly person deep into retirement.* Someone late in the retirement years should not be overly concerned with inflation and taxes eroding their returns. For many late in retirement, preservation of capital should usually be the number-one consideration for their money, and CDs are a highly worthy consideration to achieve that.

- *Short-term investing.* The need to keep your money liquid for use in the near future certainly makes investing in a CD completely justifiable.

Sheila, however, didn't fall into any of those categories. She was young; she needed higher returns for income, but solving her desire to get a higher return while keeping her money safe posed its own unique set of challenges. No matter how much I educated her on the value of dividend stocks or how a well diversified investment portfolio of stock indexes and individual bonds via a ladder would ease her concern, she just couldn't stomach any part of investing into *anything* that could cause harm to her money.

Any good advisor should naturally take this acute fear into strong consideration. Why talk about the value of diversification in a stock portfolio when the end result is going to be a person who either would ultimately never do such a thing or, if they did do such a thing, would end up being, quite frankly, a nervous wreck at the very first sign of any bump in the market?

Unfortunately, when it comes to trying to get higher rates of return while keeping an eye on complete safety, there are not many options to consider. The short list is:

- Bond ladders consisting of corporate, municipal or government bonds, which we've discussed.
- Annuities.

- Structured products; such as one type of structured product often referred to as a "Growth CD."

We have already spent quite a bit of time exploring bonds. Let's now spend a few moments taking a closer look at something few people are aware of, something that is occasionally referred to as a Growth CD.

CDs That Pay 10 Percent

Back in the bad market years, many people pulled their money out of the markets and placed it in cash. Afraid of investing in the markets again, they went searching for new products, one of which was the index annuity, which attracted quite a few risk-adverse investors for reasons previously discussed.

As investors started pulling their money out of cash and investing it with insurance companies offering index annuities, many banks scratched their heads, wondering how they were going to attract this money back into their pockets.

In some cases, the answer led the banks to essentially replicate the concept of an index annuity, but within the framework of a CD.

This brings up an interesting area of the CD market that many investors have never heard about. The area of the market I am referring to is technically entitled "structured products." Many people, however, refer to one area of them as "growth CDs." For purposes of clarity, I'm going to use this latter name instead of the more technical "structured product" counterpart.

A so-called growth CD offers the same safety as a regular bank CD: safety, Federal Deposit Insurance Corporation (FDIC) protection, and a predetermined length of time until maturity.

The big difference is that in a regular bank CD, you know exactly how much interest you're going to earn before investing in it. It's a "bird in the hand" investment. Regardless of whether it's a three-month or five-year CD, you know exactly what you're going to get: maybe it's 5 percent for one year, 7 percent for seven years, and so on.

The interest you receive on a growth CD, however, is not determined by interest rates. Similar to the way index annuities calculate their rate of return, the potential earnings on a growth CD is determined by a stock market index, such as the S&P 500 or various foreign indexes.

If the S&P 500 goes up, then you will presumably earn more interest than the "bird in the hand" bank CD. But if the S&P 500 goes down in value *and* you hold your CD until maturity (typically three to five years on average), you at least get your money back. Some growth CDs not only guarantee you'll get your money back, but they also provide a small amount of interest even if the market goes down.

Keep in mind: If you break the growth CD prior to maturity, you will get fair market value for it, which could be less than the amount you invested. But again, if held to maturity, the assurance you have in these CDs is that in the worst-case scenario, you will at least get your money back.

As for taxes, the interest on a growth CD is still taxable, just like on a bank CD. But let's assume Sheila invests in a growth CD and because of a strong stock market, she hypothetically receives 10 percent per year for the three years she is invested in it. With these types of earnings, no one would be able to rightfully call these CDs "certificates of *depreciation*."

Don't expect to go into your local bank and ask about growth CDs or structured products. Ask someone at the bank for these types of CDs and they will likely not have any idea what you are talking about. These types of CDs are offered by some of the most reputable banks in the world but are available only through various brokerage accounts. Structured products or growth CDs are a highly specialized area of the market, and many financial advisors and brokers have not heard of these investments. Unfortunately, many people are missing out on what could be a worthy inclusion in their diversified portfolios, especially those who are still young like Sheila and want to keep their money safe but also want the possibility of earning more interest than the conventional bank CDs offer.

At the time of this writing, some growth CDs have yielded impressive returns over these past few years, posting gains of well over 10 percent due to an attractive market. Needless to say, as with any stock market–driven investment, there are no guarantees that these gains will continue for any length of time, if at all. But if the concept sounds interesting to you, be sure to consult your advisor to get some more information to determine whether growth CDs make sense for a portion of your money.

Many investors want to participate in the real estate market—and with good reason. Complementary to the other reliable return investments we've discussed during the course of this chapter, real estate can produce reliable rates of return as well.

Real estate undoubtedly diversifies a portfolio of stocks, bonds, and cash. Although past performance is no guarantee of future results, over many years, the real estate sector has traditionally performed quite well.

How well? After 2001, low mortgage rates fueled a boom in the real estate market. Unless you've been hiding for the past five years or so, you might have heard of many self-made millionaire real estate investors who were popping up all around the country.

With this explosion of growth and speculation, it should come as no surprise that at the time of this writing, the "irrational exuberance" of the residential real estate market has quickly gone belly-up in many areas of the country.

Does that mean one should stay out of this sector?

No way. Diversification combined with the art of rebalancing contains the fundamental assumption that there is never really such thing as a bad market sector. Quite the contrary; diversifying and rebalancing a portfolio recognizes that every "bad child" is destined to awaken into a "good child"; we just aren't sure exactly when that's going to happen.

Even with the downturn of the residential real estate sector, real estate in general will likely always remain a fundamental ingredient of many diversified portfolios. It is for that reason, along with the art of rebalancing, that even at the time of this writing where residential real estate is generally believed to be a cold sector, it should certainly not be ignored.

Furthermore, as a reminder, remember something very important: At the time of this writing, the residential real estate sector has finally got itself through a pronounced downturn. But does that assume *all* real estate sectors are now good? Of course not. Real estate is merely one department in the financial supermarket store, while subsections within the real estate department most certainly exist.

With that, even during this bad downturn of the residential housing sub sector within the real estate asset class, there are still many other subsections that are doing quite well, such as commercial real estate properties.

Does that mean you should try to go out to buy a piece of real property? Not exactly, although needless to say, you most certainly could (even with your IRA money, which I'll be discussing later on). But real estate certainly isn't easy to invest in; analyzing the market can be quite tricky. Furthermore, purchasing investment properties yourself usually requires significant capital, time, money, and the possible frustration of having to deal with fixing someone's hair clogged sink.

While you might very well wind up purchasing a property to represent the real estate slice of a diversified portfolio, investing in real estate is an entire subject unto itself. Many investors find it difficult to understand real estate investing, and as such, the difficulty of investing in the real estate market in part led Congress to enact a law in 1960 providing for the creation of real estate investment trusts (REITs).

Real Estate Investment Trusts

REITs are companies dedicated to owning and sometimes operating income-producing real estate such as apartments, shopping centers, offices, and warehouses. Essentially, REITs allow investors to participate in the benefits of owning larger-scale real estate—often high-quality commercial properties—which tend to be less volatile than the residential real estate market, especially during a tricky time period such as the one we're now in at the time of this writing.

There are two basic types of REITs: public and private. The major difference is that public REITs are just that, publicly owned and traded on the major exchanges; one can buy and sell at any time. Not so with private REITs. Let's look at what this means in more detail.

Regulation: Public REITs must comply with the requirements of the Sarbanes-Oxley Act, including quarterly financial reporting. This leads to a certain degree of financial transparency that some investors feel adds security to the investment. Private REITs, by contrast, are required to do little in the way of disclosure, other than file an initial offering registration with the Securities and Exchange Commission.

Here is a summary of REIT characteristics:

- *Volatility.* Because they aren't exchange-traded, private REITs aren't subject to the daily fluctuations of the market as public REITs are. Typically, a private REIT intends on either going public one day or selling off its properties. Either way, at the time the shares go public (get listed and offered on the stock market exchanges for trading) or the properties within the REIT are sold off, at some point in time, the intention of a private REIT is for the investors to have an exit strategy that will allow them to cash out at some point in the future.

- *Liquidity.* Investors can readily buy and sell public REITs over the exchanges, which is not the case with private REITs. Redemptions for a private REIT are generally not permitted until two or three years after the date of the initial investment, if at all, and are usually offered at the par price (the price at which the security was issued). Private REITs may even restrict investor redemptions.

- *Dividends.* Private REITs have historically yielded dividends of 7 percent to 8 percent, compared with only 5 percent to 6 percent for public REITs.

- *Purchases.* Private REITS are purchased via a private offering memorandum through a licensed securities broker. Public REITs can be purchased through your broker or direct through any number of discount brokerages. You can invest directly in REITs or buy shares of a fund that invests in REITs. It is a good idea, however, to engage a financial advisor to help with the purchasing decision. Factors that should be evaluated when investing in REITs include:

- The geography and type of properties the REIT holds.
- The economics of those properties.
- The experience and expertise of the management team.
- The financial terms of the REIT investment.
- Your individual financial circumstances and goals.
- Fees and redemption clauses.

Like most securities, public REITs have historically experienced cyclical ups and downs. Typically, they have performed poorly when interest rates have gone up, but that is most certainly not always the case.

A dip in the market shouldn't necessarily worry potential investors. You can still reap the benefits of REITs while minimizing your risk in a number of ways. First, you can invest in REITs in certain sectors. There is an enormous variety of REITs available of all different flavors—there are REITs for prison properties, government properties, apartments, trailer parks, leisure properties, resorts, or even regional REITs (a good resource on investing in REITs is located at www.nareit.com, the National Association of Real Estate Investment Trusts web site).

It is also important to consider the quality of a REIT's management, tenants, and underlying properties. BioMed Realty Trust, for instance, specializes in leasing laboratory space to tenants such as biotechnology and pharmaceutical companies. If you believe that there will be growth in the health care sector, which many people do, it may make sense to compliment that belief with a REIT such as BioMed Realty Trust that could possibly also do well (please don't take this is as recommendation—I use BioMed merely as an example).

As with all asset classes you are considering as part of your diversified portfolio, I typically recommend you use an *index* to represent the asset class or subclass, and not an individual company—no matter how strong it appears.

Many REITs have outperformed CDs over the past decade. However, real estate is one of the most cyclical investments of all and many experts now believe that real estate has hit a cyclical peak in value.

After the last real estate valuation peak, home values fell by 30% to 50% in dozens of states across America.

Real estate crashes lead to an increasing number of mortgage delinquencies, foreclosures and banking failures. In the most recent real estate crash, dozens of banks and savings and loans encountered massive losses they incurred on mortgages and repossessed real estate. Homeowners and real estate investors lost more than $1 trillion.

Real estate prices today are much higher than they were even at the peaks in the 1990's. While the returns of some real estate investment trusts still look good, other REITs have fallen by 20% or more in value. This is a cause for concern considering that real estate is still at an all-time high. Even a minor correction in the real estate market could lead to multi-billion dollar losses for REIT investors. With millions of baby-boomers retiring and selling large houses they no longer need or want, one wonders how much longer the real estate run-up can last.

The smaller generation born after the baby-boomers is not nearly large enough to absorb all the housing stock that baby-boomers will be selling. In addition, new homes are being built at an all-time record pace. The laws of supply and demand indicate that a housing glut may be in the making.

It is also important to remember that while the returns of some REITs are still good, they are subject to taxation at your highest tax rate. REIT dividends do not enjoy the low rates at which stock dividends are taxed.

Many investors searching for reliable returns often look toward bonds to satisfy the desire. But bonds aren't the only way investors can obtain reliable returns. Certain stocks provide viable features as well.

"Stocks?" you might ask.

Yes, some stocks. Preferred stocks, for example. There are also dividend-paying stocks that we'll discuss in the next section. But preferred stocks are closer in concept to bonds, which we just discussed, so we'll start with them here.

Preferred Stocks Defined

Investing in preferred stock, like common stock, means you have ownership in a publicly held corporation. Yet preferred stockholders are in a different class, which generally gives them priority over common stockholders when it comes to earnings and assets in the event of a bankruptcy. If the company goes bankrupt, preferred stock dividends are paid *after* interest to those holding bonds but before dividends on the company's common stock.

That level of security isn't the only reason to invest in preferred stocks, however. They can also be a worthy element within a diversified portfolio designed to generate reliable returns. That's because just like a bond, preferred stocks have a stated dividend (yield), which must be paid before dividends are distributed to those who hold common stock. Dividends typically range from 5 percent to 9 percent per year and are paid quarterly or monthly. And many preferred stocks are eligible for the attractive 15 percent tax rate on dividends, preferred stocks issued by real estate investment trusts (REITs) being the notable exception. So if you're looking for less volatility than dividend stocks and a higher cash return with generally more liquidity than bonds, preferred stocks are certainly worth considering.

How do you know the stock listed is a preferred stock? If you're interested in seeing an example, check out the local newspaper's business section. Many papers list preferred stocks in a separate category. You can also look at Yahoo! Finance or CNBC. On Yahoo! Finance, preferred stocks are listed by the ticker symbol of the issuing company, followed by an underscore, followed by the letter P, followed by the series letter (if there is one, and there probably is, because companies that issue preferred stocks often have more than one series and use letters of the alphabet to distinguish them). In some places, such as tickers on CNBC, preferred stocks are listed by the company ticker symbol, followed by a vertical PR, followed by a letter indicating the specific issue.

As with any investment, some preferred stocks are better quality than others. One way to determine the quality is by looking at the stock's rating. Similar to bonds, preferred stocks are rated by Standard & Poor's and Moody's. Although the agencies use different scales, the general rule of thumb is much like a school report card:

You want to get an A, and the more As the better. Anything below a B grade is not very good in terms of credit quality.

It's a good idea, however, to know a little more about what you're buying before you dive in. So once you find a preferred stock you think you like or your advisor is recommending, take a look at the details and get down to business. It's important to understand what the company issuing the stock does, just as you would want to before buying any stock. But you also need to do a risk analysis just like you would do with bonds. In other words, how likely is it that the company will not be able to pay its preferred dividends?

Analyzing this can be pretty tricky stuff, and it's for this reason that when investing in preferred stocks, many investors will often turn to mutual funds or closed-end funds to have a manager make the selection.

For the curious minded or techie out there looking to understand how risky it is that the company might not be able to pay its preferred dividends, one way to figure that out it is to determine something called the coverage ratio. If you're in the mood to get technical or are having a difficult time falling asleep, figuring out a preferred stock's coverage ratio should help to satisfy either desire.

To calculate the coverage ratio, you divide the company's earnings before interest, taxes, depreciation, and amortization (EBITDA) by interest expense plus preferred dividends. The higher the coverage ratio, the better the chance for success. These numbers can typically be found on web sites such as Yahoo! Finance and many other places.

Of course, that may be more work than most investors want to do, and I certainly can't blame them. This is where a financial advisor usually comes in handy. He or she can help you analyze a company's risk of default and answer a number of other key questions about investing in preferred stock. For example, are the dividends cumulative? Are the shares redeemable, and if so, when? What is the likelihood of redemption? These are all key technical terms that many Main Street investors most likely aren't familiar with, which is perfectly understandable.

Another key detail to understand: the maturity date, which on preferred stocks can often be quite lengthy. Similar to a bond, preferred stocks do have a maturity date, and those dates are sometimes very far off in the distant future. As much as you can, stay away from the long maturities—just like a bond, the higher interest rates go up, the more the value on the preferred will drop.

What does this all mean?

Putting all the technical stuff aside that few people will take time to analyze (which I can completely understand, given the complexity) let me try to shed some light on this stuff for you.

Preferred stocks are often used for the portion of a portfolio that is seeking reliable returns, especially for the income-hungry investor. Without a doubt, they can make a worthy addition to a well-diversified investment portfolio.

However, a long time ago someone told me to watch out for the "heads I win, tails you lose" type of game that is sometimes found in the preferred stock world. Here's why.

Heads I Win, Tails You Lose

Many preferred stocks have what's known as a long maturity date. If you recall the previous section on bonds, the maturity date simply means that as long as the company doesn't default, maturity is the date you get your money back. By "long" maturity dates, I'm often talking *really long.*

It is not uncommon to see a maturity date on a preferred stock as far in the future as the year 2095. With these very long maturity dates that some preferred stocks have, chances are decent that the maturity dates aren't going to mean a whole heck of a lot, given that if you are reading this book, there's probably a very likely chance you won't live to see that date.

Therefore, in the absence of a shorter maturity date, when it comes to safety of our principal, this leaves our investment at the mercy of rising and falling interest rates that will constantly affect the value of our preferred stock.

Remember the two kids on the seesaw named Value and Interest Rate? As one goes up, the other goes down. And, you might also recall that in general, the longer the seesaw, the greater the fluctuations in value. Lastly, when it comes to the direction interest rates are moving, just remember this: No one really knows. It is very hard to predict the direction of interest rates.

Understanding that many preferred stocks have long maturity dates, let's return to the "heads I win, tails you lose" game. In this game, generally, three possible things can happen: Interest rates can stay the same, they can go up, or they can go down.

If interest rates stay the same, the value of a preferred stock won't fluctuate much. But let's take a look at what would happen if interest rates go up or go down— and why investing in preferred stocks can sometimes be construed as a "heads I win, tails you lose" type of game.

Scenario One: Interest Rates Go Up.

If interest rates go up, what happens to value? (Think: seesaw.)

Value goes down, and in the case of long-term maturities, value can potentially go *way* down.

So, let's suppose when you invested in a preferred stock you received a 7 percent yield.

Now, interest rates go up. And as a result of the rates going up, the value of your long-term preferred will very likely go down.

Given higher interest rates, you notice that you can now invest in new preferred stocks that offer, as an example, 9 percent.

Sounds good, right? But if you sold your preferred stock that was paying 7 percent, you're likely to sell it at a loss, given that its value went down. And the lower yielding preferred stock that you're looking to replace with the one providing a higher yield typically wouldn't make any sense given you would now be investing in it with less money.

Therefore, in this case, when interest rates went up and you were in long-term preferred stocks, the loss would likely be far too great to sell and reinvest in the higher-returning preferred stock.

So you're stuck. Painted in the corner. You lose.

Okay, next possible scenario:

Scenario Two: Interest Rates Go Down. This time, interest rates go down. What happens to value?

Value goes up, right? Right.

So, suppose you invested in a preferred stock that pays 7 percent.

Interest rates go down, so, value starts to go up.

You're happy because you presumably aren't losing any money—the underlying value of your preferred stock is trending up, and, better yet, you locked in a 7 percent rate of return on what could be a very long-term investment.

So far, so good, right? Well, here's where the "tails you lose" scenario *could* come into play:

Just when you're celebrating that you apparently locked in a 7 percent long-term rate of reliable return, all of a sudden something not so good happens, and that "something not so good" is known as a "call." A call simply means the company issuing the preferred stock is going to refinance its debt. Because interest rates went *down* and the company can now offer new preferred stock at a lower rate, it calls, or takes back the 7 percent preferred stock and gives you your money back.

You get your money out of the investment (more, less, or the same as the amount you put in, depending on a variety of circumstances). But now, with your money out of the preferred stock due to the call, can you get the same 7 percent return you just had? Chances are you won't be able to, because what happened to interest rates in this scenario?

They went down, leaving you stuck in a lower interest rate environment without being able to reproduce the reliable return you just had.

Certainly, there are many factors that can lead to deviation from the two scenarios. They are certainly not set in stone. Some preferred stocks are issued without having the possibility of a call, and a variety of other circumstances can very well make the two scenarios differ from the outcomes I outlined.

That said, these possibilities could very well occur, and in many cases are *likely* to occur. Recognizing that the maturity dates are typically very long on preferred stocks, my personal preference is to generate reliable returns by using other investment strategies, such as bond ladders and a variety of other instruments I haven't yet addressed.

But no doubt preferred stock does have its time and place in many investment portfolios, and it's for this reason I felt compelled to try to shed at least some light on what these are, how they work, and the pitfalls that could possibly exist.

Annuities: What Are They?

There are many different types of annuity products. One of the big problems I see in the marketplace is that information sources often tend to generalize annuity products and make it seem as if they are all doing the same thing. A long time ago, this may have been the case but certainly not today.

Annuities actually date back to ancient Roman times. Speculators sold financial instruments commonly known as *annua*, which translates into annual stipend or payout, which still applies to the annuity today. In ensuing years, annuities were modified to allow for enhanced payments for a specific period of years, called a term. Here in the United States in the early 1700s, the Presbyterian Church issued many annuities to new colonists concerned with outliving their money.

It used to be simple then slowly but surely things started to get a little more complex. Around two or three decades ago, companies slowly started adding more and more features to these products.

Even in my mom's days working as a full time certified financial planner, she tells me there were only a small handful of products available. Some paid income for the rest of their lives and some had a set amount of interest for a few years. And there were even a select few where you could invest in a limited amount of mutual funds within an annuity framework itself.

These days, however, choices are far more abundant and as a result, annuities can cause much confusion.

So to begin with, I'll start with a quick summary explaining the different types of annuities.

Immediate
- An irrevocable single deposit in exchange for lifetime income
- Access to income, not principal
- For money outside an IRA, tax advantaged income in the early years

Fixed
- Safe from market loss
- Earnings:

- Could be a steady interest rate for the duration of term (fixed),

- Earnings could be subject to a rate change over the course of the term (variable),

- In some cases, earnings could be *linked* to a market index (indexed)

• Tax deferred earnings

• At a cost, various riders can add additional features to the contract

Variable

• Direct investments into mutual funds (technically called "sub accounts")

• Earnings determined by market gains or losses

• Tax deferred earnings

• At a cost, various riders can add additional features to the contract

Although all share some similar characteristics, as you'll soon see, each is quite different from one another.

Immediate Annuity

If you've ever heard someone say something like, "Put your money into an annuity and you'll never see it again," they were referring to something called an *immediate annuity*.

Think that sounds scary? I can't blame you. But if you're worried about running out of money and looking for ***income you cannot outlive***, you've come to the right place.

To conceptually explain what an immediate annuity is, I'm going to use the word *pension*, but remember: an immediate annuity is ***not*** a pension in the legal sense of the word. I use it only because the concept is familiar to most and using it here merely helps illustrate the point.

Pensions: Lump Sum or Income for Life?

Retirees are sometimes faced with a decision: do they take the money they've saved in a retirement plan as a single lump sum or do they convert it to a lifetime pension?

Take it as a lump sum and it's up to the individual to invest it, generate income from it, and hope they don't outlive it. Convert it to a pension and the company assumes that responsibility. If converted to a pension, the retiree no longer has direct access to their retirement plan cash.

In concept, an immediate annuity is a similar vehicle.

At retirement, one presumably has a pile of money saved up and are faced with a choice: do they invest it, figure out how much income that can be taken from it, and work hard to make sure they don't outlive it or do they take a portion of it and create their own pension by taking out an immediate annuity?

The amount of income that can be generated from an immediate annuity largely depends on a person's age. Typically, the younger they are the less money they're going to receive. An insurance company is guaranteeing income for life so the company is certainly going to pay less to the younger person when compared to someone who is older.

Other factors that also determine the amount of income generated from the immediate annuity include interest rates, the company issuing the policy, and of great importance, the structure of the income.

The more common structures people tend to follow if funding an immediate annuity includes:

STRUCTURE	DEFINITION	ADVANTAGE	DISADVANTAGE
Life only	Income for life ending at death.	Highest income of all choices.	Income ends at death of owner.
Joint and Survivor	Surviving spouse continues to receive income at a chosen amount (for example, 100%, 75%, or 50% of the income initially received)	Income for two lives	Income ends at death of both spouses
Life with period certain	Income for life. If one dies before the chosen number of years (for example, ten years), an heir continues to receive payments up until the guaranteed years.	Early death provides heirs with income	Reduced income compared to the life only option; the longer the period, the lower the income
Life with installment refund	Income for life ending at death; if amount contributed is not returned, balance paid to heirs	Ensures amount contributed is returned to someone	Reduced income compared to other options

Inflation

One common negative heard about immediate annuities is the effect inflation has on its steady income stream. Suppose the income I initially receive is perfectly acceptable but looking ahead, will that income have the same purchasing power as it does today?

Certainly not. As such, some companies offer immediate annuities with inflation-

> A little known fact about immediate annuities: if one is in poor health, some companies will pay increased income. A medical exam is required.

adjusted income. While this might sound appealing, in most cases buyer beware: immediate annuities offering inflation-adjusted income will often start with a reduced amount of income when compared to initiating an immediate annuity *without* inflation protection.

If an immediate annuity is initiated, I often advise hedging against inflation by adding an additional immediate annuity in the future or better yet, simply supplementing the annuity income with monies from other sources such as a brokerage account.

Taxes

If money outside an individual retirement account (IRA) is used to fund an immediate annuity, the income will receive considerable tax benefits for a period of time.

In the early years of receiving the income, as documented in the Internal Revenue Service (IRS) Publication 939, the IRS deems the majority of the income received as a return of principal that was used to fund the account. The technical term for this is called the *annuity exclusion ratio rule*. In layman terms, this simply means the majority of the income received in the early years is tax-free because the IRS deems it a return of your own money that you already paid tax on.

Over time, however, the money used to fund the annuity is gradually reduced, eventually leaving nothing but interest being paid. At that point in time, typically at your life expectancy, most (if not all) of the income is taxable at ordinary income tax rates.

If IRA money is used to fund an immediate annuity, there is no exclusion. As with all money coming from an IRA, the income is *always* fully taxable at ordinary income tax rates regardless if it's coming from an annuity, mutual fund, stock, bond, certificate of deposit (CD), or other.

THE PRIVATE PENSION AND THE GENIUS BEHIND A PEANUT BUTTER AND JELLY SANDWICH

You may find this a bit "nutty," but to begin the discussion of the Private Pension, I can't help but compare it to what I truly believe is one of mankind's greatest creations; yes, the one, the only ... peanut butter and jelly sandwich.

Who was the person—as bold as Einstein, as clever as Da Vinci—to invent the legendary PB&J? What forward-thinking genius brought us this delicious treat, this ingenious sandwich that also serves as a great example of why "the whole is often far greater than the sum of its parts"? A history lesson about the visionary who invented

174

the PB&J is unfortunately far beyond the premise of this book, so for now let's focus on the sandwich itself and what it means in terms of generating highly attractive reliable returns when in retirement.

Alone, peanut butter and jelly are merely two separate jars of everyday, somewhat ordinary food products. But together in a sandwich, they are eternal soul mates, a true match made in heaven.

Similarly, for those of you currently in retirement, there are two investment products you most likely have not ever considered for yourself. But just like PB&J, together these investments could create the greatest income sandwich an income-hungry belly has ever had.

Before I tell you about more about the Private Pension, let's briefly recap some of the places where someone in retirement might consider getting reliable income while keeping their money generally safe.

- *Certificates of deposit.* CDs certainly are safe. But between a CD's typical low interest rates and taxes on the earnings, you'll protect your principal, but you might starve while doing so. If you invest $100,000 in a five-year CD, although far fetched at the time of this writing, suppose you'll earn around 5 percent, or $5,000 a year. But if you're in the 28 percent tax bracket, after taxes you'll net only around $3,600. Furthermore, the increased taxable income could push someone in retirement into a higher tax bracket and possibly affect his or her Social Security taxation as well.

- *Bonds.* Sure, you'll likely get your money back at the maturity date, but to get any reasonable rate of return, you might have to hold some bonds longer than you'd want. A bond ladder might be an excellent consideration, but sometimes, especially at the time of this writing, the yield on many good credit quality bonds remains quite low.

- *The stock market.* While dividends, preferred stocks, real estate investment trusts (REITs) and other investments can indeed offer attractive reliable returns, these are not considered to be safe investments. Furthermore, many people in retirement are looking for the simplest, safest and most effortless way to generate reliable returns, especially when it comes to generating retirement income.

Therefore, to get reliable returns, you sometimes need to be creative. Think outside the box. Be imaginative. And that's where the Private Pension comes into play.

The peanut butter side of the Private Pension is something called an *immediate annuity*. To remind you, an immediate annuity is essentially an investment contract with an insurance company that provides you with a guaranteed pension for the rest of your life.

Consider, for example, my friend Bill, who is 77 years young. The laws of probability say he can easily live another 10+ years, and when I first met him, Bill's belly was hungry, really hungry, for reliable, attractive and effortless income. After we explored various options inside the Bloomingdale's department store of investments, Bill fell in love with the Private Pension and decided it was what he wanted, so he invested his $100,000 in an immediate annuity.

In exchange for this one-time deposit, Bill gets a lifetime income stream of $12,000 per year. Throughout the remainder of Bill's life, most of the income is tax free thanks to the Internal Revenue Service (IRS) gift to investors when investing in an immediate annuity known as the "annuity exclusion ratio rule." The problem is that if Bill dies tomorrow, the income stops and his original $100,000 investment is gone, which could provide a nice return for the insurance company ... but such an event would certainly not be so good for Bill's wife, Francine.

To solve the problem of Francine tossing me out a window when the income stops, let's switch to the other side of Bill's Private Pension. For the jelly, every year Bill removes $5,000 from the $12,000 annual income stream he receives from the immediate annuity and invests it in a life insurance policy *with a death benefit equal to the amount he used to fund the immediate annuity.* With the life insurance policy in place, Francine is assured that she'll get the $100,000 back when Bill dies and the income stops.

The difference, or in technical terms, the arbitrage, between the income the immediate annuity pays ($12,000) and the cost of the life insurance policy ($5,000) equals the amount of money Bill gets to spend for his income ($7,000).

Where else could Bill get a 7 percent return for income that's mostly tax free, never to change regardless of market conditions, with a guarantee that the original investment returns to his heirs tax-free upon his death?

We've worked with many Bills, especially during times of ultra-low interest rate environments. Some have invested thousands to create their Private Pensions, while others have done it with millions. Needless to say, you must have ample savings outside the Private Pension for various needs, especially for protection against inflation and health care considerations.

Keep in mind that age, health, and other factors will ultimately determine your bottom line and whether or not this strategy makes any sense for you. In general, the older you are or the earlier you plan it, the tastier this sandwich gets. As long as you can qualify for at least some level of universal life insurance (some people simply cannot), the numbers could work out quite well for you and your heirs.

Bonds? CDs? Stock market?

Creamy? Crunchy? Super-chunky or reduced fat?

Everyone has their own taste, but one thing is for sure: In the complex world of investments and considering the fear many have about outliving their money, this

Private Pension sandwich could be one well worth sinking your teeth into.

The Private Pension in Action

Before taking a closer look at the many ways one can design a Private Pension, let's recap Bill's plan. Remember, the math that follows is not accurate for everyone and should therefore be considered hypothetical. Exact numbers for any one person will depend on a variety of factors including, but not limited to, age, health, and the current interest rate environment. That said, before any money is ever invested into a Private Pension, all returns and insurance costs must always be well documented, guaranteed in print by the insurance companies, and, of course, well understood by the investor considering a Private Pension.

In Bill's case, the structure of his Private Pension was:

First, he invested $100,000 into an immediate annuity. This provides lifetime income of $12,000 per year, mostly tax-free. The income is locked in, never to change and will continue for the rest of life.

For many people, the understandable concern of an immediate annuity is that there is no access to the invested amount; there is only access to the income it provides. Furthermore, when the person receiving the income dies, the income ends with them and there is nothing left for heirs.

To counter that risk: First of all, one would never invest *all* their money into a Private Pension. There must be ample savings outside the plan for a wide variety of reasons (inflation and unforeseen emergencies are at the top of the list).

Next: in his case, Bill removes $5,000 a year from the $12,000 yearly income and invests it into a life insurance policy worth the same amount he used to fund his Private Pension ($100,000).

The difference between the income the immediate annuity produces and the amount that needs to be invested into the life insurance policy represents the dollars that's left for Bill to spend. This is otherwise known as an arbitrage.

In his case, this leaves Bill with a locked-in 7 percent rate of return for income that will last the rest of his life.

This amount is mostly tax-free (a tax-equivalent return of most likely over 9 percent depending on one's tax bracket); it will never change regardless of what happens to the markets or interest rates.

When he dies, the income stops *and* the $100,000 he used to fund his Private Pension is returned to his heirs through the life insurance.

Customizing the Private Pension

Let's look at a few examples on how the Private Pension can be customized to meet different desires. We'll then take a look as to why planning for this early on while in the accumulation stage can make the Private Pension much more compelling.

Scenario #1: More Income, Leave Less Money to Heirs

To increase Bill's income, he can consider leaving less money to heirs. Instead of leaving Bill's family $100,000 tax free as in the preceding example, to increase his income, he can leave them *less* death benefit:

Bill invests $100,000 in an immediate annuity that produces a 12 percent return, providing him with a guaranteed lifetime income of $12,000 a year.

He then uses some of this income to purchase a life insurance policy not worth $100,000 as earlier, but less—for example, $75,000—upon his death. Because he is leaving less death benefit, the amount invested into the insurance will also be less. As an example, leaving $75,000 would require not $5,000, but $3,500 per year.

With less money invested in his insurance, Bill then is left with a higher amount of spendable income. In this case, the guaranteed income for the rest of his life would not be 7 percent as earlier, but 8.5 percent, or $8,500 a year, mostly tax free.

By lowering the amount he leaves to his family, he increases his income.

Scenario #2: Less Income, Leave More Money To Heirs

What if Bill doesn't need as much income and wants to leave *more* money to heirs? In this case, he can *raise* the amount of life insurance he leaves and thereby *lower* his income.

Instead of leaving heirs $100,000 as in the original example, Bill wants to leave them more.

Bill invests $100,000 in an immediate annuity that produces a 12 percent return, providing him with a guaranteed lifetime income of $12,000 a year, mostly tax-free.

He then uses some of this income to invest in a life insurance policy worth more than $100,000. To leave heirs $125,000, he would have to spend $7,500 per year.

Bill is then left with a guaranteed income of $4,500 a year (4.5 percent return) that is mostly tax-free. This is less income than the other examples because Bill chooses to leave more money to heirs.

As you can see, there is no science to the Private Pension. The numbers are completely flexible according to one's desires. We have designed Private Pensions for people who received income (after the cost of the life insurance) of anywhere between 5 and 15 percent. It all starts with an understanding of a person's exact needs and investments and whether or not they can qualify for a universal life insurance policy at all, which brings up another important point.

Scenario #3: Bad Health

We often hear people in retirement say, "I'm not in good health. The cost of insurance would be *way* too high to make the Private Pension work."

As long as someone can qualify for *some* life insurance, the Private Pension can still work out just fine. True, bad health will cause the required investment into the insurance to be higher, but the income being produced from the immediate annuity will be higher as well. Remember:

- The *immediate annuity company* wants Bill to die right away (he gives the insurance company $100,000 and, as morbid as it sounds, the company hopes he dies immediately).

- The *life insurance company* wants Bill to live a very long time (he keeps investing money into the insurance policy every year, and the more years he invests, the more attractive it is for the life insurance company).

So if Bill placed $100,000 into an immediate annuity, the annuity company would certainly appreciate it if they paid him income for a few short years and then died. Why? Because remember: Once he dies, the income stops and the annuity company keeps the amount originally invested.

But if Bill is in bad health, to entice him to invest, what will the insurance company do? The annuity company will *increase* the amount of income he receives. In this case, let's look at another example of how this could work:

Let's suppose Bill's health isn't good, but he still wants to create a Private Pension for himself. In case of bad health, here's what the Private Pension may look like:

Bill invests $100,000 in an immediate annuity. Because he's in poor health, the annuity provides him not with a 12 percent rate of return (as in the healthy scenarios above), but, as a hypothetical example, a 15 percent rate of return, which gives him a guaranteed lifetime income of $16,000 a year. Remember: He's getting a much higher income because he's sick and the annuity company would like to think they will be paying Bill for a short period of time.

Because he's ill, the investment into his insurance will also be higher. From the higher amount of income coming from the immediate annuity, he removes the amount necessary to replace the $100,000 upon his death. In this case, the investment into the life insurance policy will be higher than $5,000 (in the scenarios when he was healthy). In this example, maybe he'll have to remove an amount as high as $9,000.

In this hypothetical example, Bill is still left with a guaranteed income of $7,000 (7 percent) a year, mostly tax free, which in this example is the same amount of income received when he was healthy. So, even if someone is not in good health, as long as they can qualify for some life insurance, the Private Pension can still possibly work in their favor.

To summarize, the Private Pension creates what's called an "arbitrage" (a spread) between the investment into the life insurance and the income the immediate annuity produces. The difference or spread between the investment into the life insurance and the income the immediate annuity generates is the Private Pension, the amount one gets to spend for the rest of their life.

Scenario #4: The benefits of planning early

For those in the accumulation stage, you may be asking, "why plan it now?"

When discussing the Private Pension with those in the accumulation stage, some will quickly dismiss it due to their young age. This is entirely true for the immediate annuity side of the Private Pension sandwich. For many reasons, it typically makes no sense at all to ever invest in an immediate annuity until you are past the age of 70.

But if the concept sounds like something you'd consider when in retirement, then along with the other benefits discussed earlier, this could be a strong reason to consider adding some life insurance to your diversified investment portfolio.

Why do it now? It's simple: The younger you are when initiating the life insurance policy, the higher the income from the Private Pension will be. For those concerned about whether or not they will have enough income at retirement, or if they will outlive it, this is truly one of the most powerful strategies to help minimize both concerns.

Let's look at an example as to why the Private Pension can be such a powerful strategy *the earlier you plan for it* by first recapping Bill's original plan:

In his 70s, Bill invests $100,000 in an immediate annuity that produces a 12 percent return, providing him with a guaranteed lifetime income of $12,000 a year.

He then uses a portion of this income to invest in a life insurance policy to replace the $100,000 upon his death. At the age he created the Private Pension (mid-70s), this requires an investment of $5,000 per year.

He then has a guaranteed net income of $7,000 (7 percent) a year, mostly tax-free.

Suppose Bill read this book while he was in the accumulation stage of his life and the concept sounded interesting. If he took out the $100,000 life insurance policy when he was in his 50s, the Private Pension later on would look much more attractive at retirement.

Fast forward to Bill now in his 70s when he's ready to begin his Private Pension. With the universal life policy in place since his 50s, he removes (in this example) $100,000 from his savings and makes a one-time deposit to fund the immediate annuity.

Having preplanned for this to happen, Bill's Private Pension may now look something like this:

Now in his 70s, Bill invests $100,000 in an immediate annuity that produces a 12 percent return, providing him with a guaranteed lifetime income of $12,000 a year, mostly tax-free.

He then uses some of this income to *continue* investing in the universal life insurance policy.

Because the life insurance was initiated when he was in his 50s, the annual investment to continue the policy could be a mere 1 percent. Remember: The earlier you take out the insurance, the less investment it will require.

In this example, Bill would only have to remove 1 percent from the immediate annuity to keep the universal life policy in force.

He is then left with a guaranteed income not of 7 percent but of 11 percent, or $11,000 per year, mostly tax-free.

By planning for the Private Pension much earlier, Bill vastly increased his annual income *for the rest of his life*. In this example, he will receive an 11 percent rate of return, mostly tax free, locked in for the rest of his life and guaranteed never to run out. If that sounds good, be sure to remember that an 11 percent mostly tax-free rate of return has an equivalent *taxable* return of 13 to 14 percent.

If you can plan now to give yourself such a high rate of return for the rest of your life and never outlive the income, wouldn't it make sense to plan for this now? If there's ever a strategy to plan for as early as possible, I hope you can see that the Private Pension is usually at the top of the list.

Double My Income at Retirement? How?

This brings me to a key point. Earlier, I claimed the Private Pension can often more than *double your income* when in retirement. How can I make that claim?

At some point in the past, you may have heard or been advised about something called "the withdrawal rate" from a retirement portfolio. As mentioned at the end of the last chapter, many advisors will prudently tell you that when you retire and start using your investments for income, you should not withdraw more than 4 to 5 percent of your portfolio per year. If you can keep your withdrawals to within these percentages, then given all historical stock and bond market data available, prudent planning says these withdrawal rates will provide you with the absolute best chances of not outliving your money.

If you understand the concept of the Private Pension, then you understand that this strategy will not only greatly increase your income, but it will also give you the assurance you won't ever outlive it.

The Private Pension is an *insurance-based* strategy that is *guaranteed* to produce the results. And, if planned for early, the amount of reliable income that can be safely produced from the Private Pension when you reach retirement years can easily be as high as 10 percent or in many cases, even higher.

Therefore, when claiming adding life insurance to your diversified investment portfolio *as soon as possible* can potentially better than double your income at retirement, this is exactly where I "put my money where my mouth is." The power of this strategy cannot be emphasized enough. The Private Pension offers:

- Highly attractive income (that typically far exceeds the recommended withdrawal rate).
- Mostly tax-free income.
- Income that you will not outlive.
- Income that is not subject to any stock market or interest rate risk.

The assurance that the amount used to fund your Private Pension will be returned to heirs tax-free.

Who says there will no longer be such thing as reliable pensions when we retire? With a Private Pension in place, such a thing will never be the case.

Did I Waste My Money?

When discussing the Private Pension with someone in the accumulation stage we'll often hear the comment, "But what happens if I never wind up initiating a Private Pension? If I don't do it later on, I wasted my money on the insurance!" That's the person speaking who sees life insurance as a *cost*. I hope by now you see it as we do, as an *investment* that has many possible benefits and exit strategies including giving yourself the opportunity to *sell it at a profit* if you later have no use for it.

Many people in their 50s start to actively plan for retirement. Would it not be smart at such an age to also start planning how one is going to get the most amount of reliable income in retirement with the least amount of risk *and* the assurance that you will never outlive your money?

The Private Pension and IRAs

Until now, the income the Private Pension generates is mostly tax free, and that's certainly an attractive benefit. This assumes the Private Pension is funded with after-tax dollars outside a qualified account such as an IRA.

But designing a Private Pension using IRA money could make sense as well. Here's why:

When an IRA was originally conceived, what was it designed to do? Be used for income in retirement, correct? For various reasons, using your IRA money to create a Private Pension could very well be the best of all alternatives.

Imagine for a moment that you are in your 70s and in retirement. Now it's time to use your IRA for the reason it was created in the first place: to give you income. After many years of accumulating money in their IRAs, many retirees we meet are looking for a simple and safe way to generate reliable income, especially the kind they cannot outlive.

Many people we meet in retirement withdraw only the required minimum distributions from of their IRAs. When an IRA is passed to the next generation, as mentioned earlier, many heirs cash out the IRA and as a result would very likely wind up paying a lot of tax.

So, if generating an attractive income stream you cannot outlive *and* passing the value of your IRA tax free to heirs both sound interesting, you may want to consider using all or a portion of your IRA money to create the Private Pension.

Here's a hypothetical example:

Suppose I have an IRA worth $100,000. Also assume I have plenty of money outside the IRA. With the IRA money, I invest in an immediate annuity that provides a lifetime income of $13,000 a year.

I use some of this income to invest in a life insurance policy that provides $100,000 at death. Hypothetically, suppose a $100,000 death benefit requires an annual investment of $6,000. Removing this amount from the yearly income leaves me with a guaranteed $7,000 per year.

Now, for the rest of my life, I have an income stream of 7 percent being generated from my original investment of $100,000.

At death, the income dies with me and there's nothing left to heirs.

Except, however, remember: I was removing $6,000 per year to invest in the life insurance policy worth $100,000 when I die.

Therefore, when I die, the heirs get the $100,000 value of my IRA *not* fully taxable, but *tax-free*. This is because the *value* of my IRA is inherited in the form of a life insurance policy's tax-free death benefit.

With this planning, I receive a guaranteed income that I cannot outlive and my heirs receive the full value of my IRA not taxable, but tax-free.

Needless to say, taxes and a variety of other issues have to be factored in to determine whether or not using IRA money to fund a Private Pension would make sense given your own personal needs.

Immediate Annuities: Summary

An immediate annuity is an irrevocable contract between an owner and an insurance company that guarantees lifetime income in exchange for a single deposit. The amount of income received primarily depends on:

- Age
- Current and projected interest rates, and
- The income structure chosen such as:
  - Life only: provides the most amount of income because upon death, the income   stops.
  - Joint and Survivor: Surviving spouse continues receiving the same amount of income or less depending on the choice selected when the annuity was initiated.

- Period certain: income for life but if death takes place before the end of the period (for example, ten years), an heir continues receiving the income up until the balance of years is complete.

DEFERRED ANNUITIES

Deferred annuities include:

- Fixed
  - Indexed
  - Hybrid

- Variable

In deferred annuities the money contributed into them presumably grows over time during what's commonly referred to as the *deferral* or *accumulation* stage.

In effect, the owner is letting their money grow and then deferring its conversion into an immediate annuity. Technically, converting money built up over time into an immediate annuity is called *annuitization* but don't be alarmed. If the immediate annuity concept is not something that interests the owner, with rare exception, most deferred annuities do not require annuitization. It is merely an option.

> Before entering into a deferred annuity, always be sure to ask "does this annuity require me to annuitize? Most deferred annuities do not require it but it's always a good idea to double check

In fact, most insurance companies report the vast majority of people do not annuitize their contracts. Most people simply keep their money in the deferred stage and at some point in the very near or distant future they simply take periodic withdrawals when needed.

Funding a deferred annuity is accomplished either by depositing money all at once or over time, known as *flexible premium* policies. Some deferred annuities allow only an initial deposit and do not accept additional contributions.

Differences

The differences between annuities such as fixed, indexed, and variable can be enormous but there is one element they share in common: tax deferral. Before going through the differences, let's take a closer look at this common trait.

According to the IRS, there are basically two types of money:

- Money that has not been taxed yet and, of course,
- Money that has been taxed

In the IRS' eyes, money that has not been taxed is called *qualified*, which exists in places such as 401(k)s and IRAs; money that has already been taxed is called *non-qualified*, which could exist in any number of places such as bank accounts, brokerage accounts, and other.

Taxes on Qualified Money

In accounts such as 401(k)s, IRAs, and similar vehicles such as simplified employee pension (SEP) IRAs, money has been received

> Questions about taxes? Always refer them to your accountant or CPA. He or she is the only person qualified to address these concerns.

but as the account presumably grows in value, taxes are not owed until the owner takes money out.

In layman terms, taxes are not owed until the owner takes money out is a reasonable way to describe the concept of tax deferment. Whether the account is growing as a result of interest being earned, stocks going up in value, or any number of other ways, there's no taxes owed until the owner withdraws money from the account.

If the owner doesn't take money out, then when one turns seventy and a half years old, the IRS forces the owner to take money out via required minimum distributions (RMD). If the owner ignores these RMD requirements, the IRS will penalize the owner with additional taxes and penalties.

When money comes out of these accounts, it's taxed as ordinary income, meaning, the IRS deems it as income received. In most cases, taxation on income exposes the money to the highest of all possible tax rates. At the time of this writing, depending on one's tax rate, ordinary income can incur taxes as high as 39 percent and even higher after state and local taxes are applied.

Money can be taken out of these accounts at any time but if it's taken before the age of fifty-nine and a half not only will taxes be owed, but the owner will also incur additional penalties of 10 percent and sometimes even more.

There are a few ways to potentially avoid these penalties and I'll address a few after some words about money outside of IRA/401(k) type of vehicles called non-qualified accounts.

Taxes on Non-Qualified Accounts

Taxes on non-qualified accounts are a different animal. When investing non-qualified money, the company holding your money will in most cases issue a 1099 tax report that shows earnings exposed to taxes such as:

- Interest earned from CDs
- Interest earned from bonds
- Gains and losses from sales of various investments
- Dividends earned from individual stocks

• Dividends and/or interest earned from mutual funds

The IRS taxes these earnings differently than IRAs and 401(k)s:

- • Interest earned from CDs is taxable as ordinary income (same as IRAs)
- • Interest earned from corporate bonds are also taxed as ordinary income. Municipal bonds are tax-free at the federal level and if the bond is purchased in one's home state, they are deemed tax-free at the state and local level as well; AMT tax could apply

- • Gains and losses from the sales of stocks are taxed either as ordinary income (gains on a stock sold within a year of purchasing them) or long term capital gains (between 15 and 20 percent)

- • Dividends and/or interest earned from individual stocks are taxed as either ordinary income taxes and/or dividend tax between 15 and 20 percent

As one can see, when investing non-qualified money, the owner has some control and choices as to how their investments are taxed whereas when investing in qualified accounts such as IRAs, the owner **has no choice**.

Annuities to the Rescue?

As you can see, with the possible exception of muni bonds, all the above investments will incur at least some tax.

To avoid paying any taxes on non-qualified money, some people search for ways to minimize or get rid of the taxes. Some will invest in munis, some will make additional contributions to a 401(k) or IRAs, and some will use annuities as the solution to defer tax.

Once monies are placed in a deferred annuity, interest and/or dividends earned are not taxed until this money is taken out. The nice part of this is that it is in the owner's control when taxes are paid, not as a result of 1099s.

In addition to controlling when one pays taxes, another key benefit of tax deferment is that all money remains in the account left to compound. When investing in the products previously listed, money is typically compounding off a lower amount given that in most cases, taxes are often owed each year.

Albert Einstein called compounding interest the eighth wonder of the world because the mathematical advantage it provides. I promised I would not use much math in this book, so I'm going to avoid it here but if you're interested in understanding the concept of compounding interest and how powerful it is, Google it and you'll have more examples of it than you care to know.

The Downside of Tax Deferment

Often, companies that market annuities and the advisors who promote them are very quick to point out the power of tax deferment and compounding interest. While there's no doubt there are benefits to each, there's also an important potential disadvantage that I believe does not get addressed nearly enough.

At first glance not paying taxes until you decide to take money out appears to be a great thing. The account owner is in full control of when they pay tax and no taxes are owed until then. That's fantastic on its face. But one needs to understand what happens when the money is taken from a tax deferred vehicle such as a deferred annuity—it's at that point earnings are taxed the same way qualified (IRA) money is taxed: at ordinary income tax rates.

Remember: ordinary income taxes expose money to the highest of all possible taxes. Depending on your tax rate, it can be as low as 10 percent but as high as 39 percent.

So when funding an annuity with non-qualified money, even though taxes are deferred, one needs to understand that much like an IRA, deferring the taxes could result in higher taxes when compared to taxation on other investments.

Younger Investors

I'm often asked if an annuity is advisable for younger investors. It's really not the age; it's the mindset. A person I help in his eighties is quick to say he feels as if he's still a very young investor. But for arguments sake, I'll deem a younger investor as someone in their thirties or forties. (For the record, I'm in my late forties and still trying to think of myself as a young investor.)

Without knowing a person's unique financial situation and goals, it's impossible to say whether or not a younger investor should consider an annuity. That said, for those in their younger years, there's one very important point to understand: if a person funds an annuity, the earnings are tax deferred but—and this is a big but—if earnings are withdrawn before turning fifty-nine and a half, then just like withdrawals from an IRA, those earnings will be taxed *and* they'll incur IRS penalties as well of 10 percent or more.

So, if someone younger than fifty-nine and a half funds an annuity with non-qualified or qualified money, they really need to understand that in order to avoid penalties on earnings they'll have to wait until after they're fifty-nine and a half years old to take them. If they plan on using this money before that age, or are unsure if they will need it, then an annuity is most likely not the product they should consider.

Using Qualified Money to Fund Annuities

Using qualified money (IRA) to fund an annuity is different because any money taken from an IRA before the age of fifty-nine and a half will always incur taxes and penalties *unless* one of the IRS allowable exceptions are met including:

- Disability
- Inherited IRA
- Home purchase
- 72-T (substantially equal periodic payments)

I once read that funding an annuity with IRA money is like using two umbrellas in the rain because monies in an

IRA are already tax deferred. Therefore, using an annuity that is also tax deferred provides no benefit to the account owner whatsoever. While I certainly agree that using two umbrellas to use in the rain is a bit of overkill, when it comes to using IRA money to fund an annuity, in most cases I disagree with the correlation because most people I've come across have decided to use an annuity not because of tax treatments; they decided to use an annuity because of the guarantees and benefits they provide.

In fact, I'd venture to say that using an annuity inside an IRA is preferable over using money that exists outside an IRA because if one uses after-tax money outside an IRA to fund an annuity, they are replacing possible tax advantage treatments of that money in exchange for ordinary income tax, which as mentioned often exposes one to the highest of all possible taxes when compared to potentially lower taxes that could have been realized on dividends and/or capital gains.

When using IRA money to fund an annuity, regardless of whether one is using an annuity, mutual fund or anything else, withdrawals from an IRA are always taxed at ordinary income tax rates. Therefore, when funding an annuity with IRA money, one is not putting their money into a worse tax position than it already is, whereas when using money outside of an IRA, one might very well be doing such a thing.

This isn't to say one should not consider using money outside an IRA to fund an annuity. It's only to say that sometimes, using two umbrellas in the rain could indeed have practical use.

Fixed annuities are CD-like investments issued by insurance companies (but for the record, they are definitely *not* CDs). Like CDs, they pay guaranteed rates of interest typically for a pre-determined length of time.

Fixed annuities have the following key attributes:

- Safety from market loss
- Contract term and penalties for early surrender
- Penalty free withdrawals
- Fixed, variable and/or indexed rates of return

Let's take a closer look at each.

Safety from Market Loss

Money contributed into a fixed annuity is not subject to market loss. For those looking for market returns, this is definitely not a product for you. But for those looking to keep their money safe from any possibility of market loss, a fixed annuity could be something to consider.

Term and Penalties

In most cases, entering into a fixed annuity means one is agreeing to hold their money in the account for a predetermined length of time. The term might be anywhere from a few years to much longer in some cases.

YEAR	PENALTY
1	10%
2	8%
3	7%
4	6%
5	5%
6	4%
7	2%
8	0%

The term is sometimes referred to as the contract length, surrender period, or the penalty period and it's a very important concept to understand before entering into any deferred annuity.

As an example of how a term typically works, suppose I'm attracted to a fixed annuity and I see the term of the contract is seven years. What this typically means is that after the first year, if I wanted I could withdraw without penalty 10 percent of the account value each year.

However, if within seven years I withdraw more than 10 percent, I am likely going to pay a penalty, which is sometimes known as a surrender charge or early withdrawal fee.

The amount I can take penalty-free, at what point in time it can first be taken, and the surrender fees I might be subject to vary between companies and products. Generally, they're all over the map but as an example, a penalty/surrender fee schedule might appear similar to the table shown.

Using the table on the previous page, suppose in the

> If you're ever in an annuity, it's wise to call the company to find out the exact penalty-free withdrawal and surrender amount before taking any money out.

third year my account is worth $50,000. Typically, I'd be allowed to withdraw 10 percent of the account value for a total of $5,000 but monies taken over this amount will be assessed a penalty fee of 7 percent.

If in the third year, suppose I close the account and withdraw all my money. The first $5,000 would come out penalty-free but as per the schedule, the remaining $45,000 would be subject to a 7 percent penalty ($3,150). Therefore, when closing the account, I wouldn't receive $50,000 but in this example, I'd receive $46,850 due to the surrender fee.

In some contracts, the penalty is subject to a market value adjustment (MVA) where the penalty could be adjusted higher or lower than the percentage shown.

Deviances to the Penalty-Free Amount

I use 10 percent penalty-free withdrawal because it's a commonly used structure in many deferred annuity contracts. However, the penalty-free amount could easily differ in a number of ways, such as:

- Penalty-free: premium or account value?
- Cumulative withdrawals
- Return of premium
- Illness

Penalty-Free: On the Initial Contribution (Premium) or Account Value?

In most cases, the penalty-free withdrawal amount is a percentage of the account value but in rare cases, the penalty-free amount might be a percentage of the initial premium. In contracts where the penalty-free amount is based on the initial premium, the amount that can be taken is in nearly all cases less than the account value approach.

When evaluating *any* deferred annuity (fixed or variable), always be sure to ask what the penalty-free amount is based on: the account value or the initial premium?

Cumulative

Some contracts offer 10 percent penalty-free withdrawals each year and in addition, if one doesn't take a withdrawal in a given year, the unused penalty-free amount rolls over and accumulates into the following year. In such a case, if one needs to take a withdrawal in the year that follows, they would be entitled to withdraw 20 percent of the account value without penalty.

Extending this even further, some contracts continue accumulating unused penalty-free amounts for many years, typically capping it off at a certain percent such as 50 percent or more.

Return of Premium

A new feature on some hard-to-find contracts is a return of premium option that allows the owner to get all premiums paid returned at any time without any penalty or fees assessed against it.

Suppose I initiate a five-year term annuity with a single premium of $50,000. But for whatever reason, soon after I open the account I want to close it. With a return of premium option, I simply contact the company and they'd return the $50,000 premium in full.

Keep in mind: if I earned interest on the $50,000, assuming I'm still within the term of the contact, I will likely be assessed a penalty on the interest, but not the premium itself. It's a compelling feature recently added to some hard-to-find contracts and as such, I've seen some folks previously apprehensive about annuities now take a closer look.

Illness

For those requiring medical assistance, most annuities offer a significant increase to the penalty-free amount that can be taken during the term. Proof of assistance is required and is often tied to something known as activities of daily living such as bathing, dressing, eating, feeding, toilet, and mobility. For example, a contract may stipulate that as long as one needs assistance with say two of six activities of daily living, the company would permit a 50 percent penalty-free withdrawal during the term.

End of Term

I'm often asked, "What happens at the end of the term?"

> Careful! At the end of the term, some companies might automatically reset the term of your contract. Companies cannot do this without prior notice to the account owner but it's an important possibility to address.

Suppose I enter into a contract with a seven-year term and I complete the full amount of years. In most cases, this simply means there's no penalty of any kind on any withdrawal amount and the company will allow me to keep my money in the account up until the annuity maturity date, which is the date when the company has the right to force the owner to liquidate and close the account.

Keep in mind, annuity maturity dates are typically in the distant future and are not the same as the contract term.

Rates of Return

Earnings in a fixed annuity are typically determined by either a fixed, variable, or indexed return.

Fixed Return

In some policies, a contract will offer a fixed return that doesn't change during the term. At the completion of the term, the company reserves the right to adjust the rate. At that point in time, the owner can either withdraw all their money without penalty and close the account or if the adjusted rate is desirable, simply leave it in.

Variable Return

A deviance to a fixed return is when a company offers a stated return for the first year or longer and then reserves the right to adjust it after this period is complete. While at first this might seem undesirable, it could work in the owner's favor. Some companies are quick to provide renewal rate histories revealing an excellent track record of raising rates. On the flip side, however, if a company lowers the rate, most contracts guarantee a floor/minimum return.

For example, a company might offer an initial first year rate of 5 percent with a minimum of three. The worst case scenario after the first year is a 3 percent return. [1]

---

[1] I've been asked, "Am I stuck if a company lowers their rate and there are more attractive rates out there?"

There could be a way to offset penalty fees, not suffer a loss, and initiate a new annuity to take advantage of a more competitive rate. I

Indexed Return

Returns determined by a stock market index such as the Standard and Poor's 500 are otherwise known as Indexed Annuities. Although these annuities fall within the Fixed Annuity group, they deserve attention all to themselves.

---

address this further in the "1035 Exchange" and "Bonus" sections of this handbook.

INDEXED RETURNS, A/K/A INDEXED ANNUITIES

The last type of return available in some fixed annuities is not determined by the insurance company's fixed or variable rates; it's determined by stock market indexes.

If you're thinking, But the markets have risk and I can lose my money, don't despair. In these types of annuities, the principal and any prior earnings are not subject to market loss.

To describe how these annuities work, I'll illustrate the concept using a popular game of chance.

Familiar with the game of black jack? Suppose you're walking around a casino looking to play and up ahead you see two tables. At first they appear to be the same but upon closer inspection, the rules between them are quite different. The first table plays by traditional rules: beat the dealer, you win but if you lose, you lose your bet. Simple as that.

But at the second table if you beat the dealer you win a *portion* of your bet, but if the dealer wins, *you lose nothing.* In addition, if you let previous winnings ride and bet them, those winnings cannot be lost either. On this table, you're not playing *against* the dealer, rather, the dealer is your partner and I'll explain more of this in just a bit.

Sound interesting? That's why over the years fixed indexed annuities have experienced quite significant growth.

Indexed Annuities Defined

To begin with, as mentioned, an indexed annuity is just another version of a fixed annuity that determines its return not by the company but by linking the returns to the performance of a market index. The fact that returns are *not* determined at a company's discretion is sometimes enough of a reason for some folks to choose this type fixed annuity over the other types. Indexes available in these types of annuities are most often the Standard and Poor's 500 (S&P 500) along with the Dow, Russell 2000, international, and in some rare cases, even gold and commodity indexes as well.

At the inception of the contract, the account owner must choose the index (or if available, multiple indexes) they wish to link their money to. If the belief is that the market indexes won't perform well during the year ahead, there is often a one-year fixed return option as well, which

I call the bird-in-the-hand option whereas selecting an index could provide two in the bush.

The Step-Up/Annual Reset Feature

A significant feature of an indexed annuity is that earnings are locked in at each anniversary date of the contract. Should the chosen market index drop the following year, the account owner won't be credited with any interest but *earnings from prior years cannot be lost*. This is commonly referred to as the *annual reset* of an indexed annuity.

Think of a rising staircase. A chart displaying this appears level during bad market years and then steps up during favorable ones. To help understand this point, a picture is sometimes worth a thousand words. Below is one company's published indexed annuity performance. It assumes the contract owner selected the S&P 500 as the index to measure returns against and no withdrawals were taken from the account.

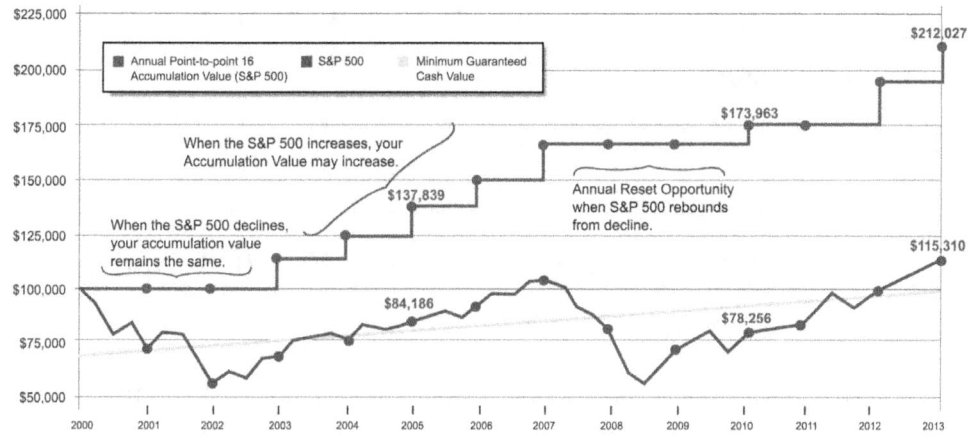

As you see, this company's indexed annuity started with $100,000 and ended with $212,027 whereas the direct investment in the S&P 500 ended with $115,318, leaving the index annuity account with nearly $100,000 more money.

While that's indeed quite a difference, I believe the most important difference is something worth far more than $100,000. It's often the *behavioral difference* between the market investor and the index annuity account owner that no chart can accurately depict.

Investor Behavior

Based on experience, an investor in the above S&P account would likely end the period with less than the amount shown.

Why?

Think about what happens during market crashes such as one in 2001 and worse, the crash of 2007-2008. During crashes such as these, it's not uncommon for investors to bail from the markets and go into cash. Once out of harm's way, the next question that soon needs to be addressed is, *When do I get back into the markets?*

Often, it's often long *after* the market starts to steadily rebound that many investors believe that the worst should be over and then start easing back in gradually. This behavior suppresses returns and shows that with very rare exception, trying to time the market hardly ever works.

In a widely publicized extensive research report entitled The Quantitative Analysis of Investor Behavior (QAIB), the nation's leading financial research firm DALBAR concluded that the majority of market investors typically average a mere 2 to 3 percent growth on their money (If interested in reading the report, visit www.qaib.com). Along with taxes and fees, the primary reason cited for such a low rate of return is investors trying to time the market; often, they go out of the market when things are bad and return only when things are appearing good.

On the other hand, the owner of the indexed annuity never has to bail out of the market given no losses can occur. If one knew they could never lose any money, they would not feel the need to ever get out of harm's way. By remaining linked to the market the entire time, an indexed annuity owner won't bail at the worst time or reinvest at the top. The money is always exposed but not at the risk of losing it.

Often, the best bull markets immediately follow the worst ones and in the case of an indexed annuity account owner, in most instances, their money is *always* ready for the next bull run.

Warren Buffet said it best: "The first rule of investing is to never lose money, and the second rule is: see rule number one."

While you might not see the big annual returns in an indexed annuity, over time there may be considerable growth above and beyond that of a typical market investor due to the inherent peace of mind that in my opinion is worth far more than the $100,000 difference above.

Does this mean everyone wanting market growth should be in an indexed annuity?

No way. There's some things we need to cover first.

Too Good to Be True?

To some, a chart such as the one above appears too good to be true but remember, there's no such thing as a free lunch. If you enter into an indexed annuity, you are going to give up a few things.

- **Loss of liquidity**: as previously mentioned, when entering into an annuity, unless one has a return of premium option, they will pay a penalty if the account is *fully* terminated before the term is complete. Frankly, while I don't ever advocate terminating a contract, if someone ever had to do it and pay a penalty, at least they are in control of their loss as opposed to a market investment controlling it for them.

- **Limiting gains:** although in the previous chart over time the indexed annuity outperformed the actual S&P 500, on an *annual* basis most indexed annuities have limits on what they can earn. In an indexed annuity, money is not directly invested in the market index. The performance of the market index merely acts as the measurement of returns one receives that is often subjected to a limit, or cap.

The Cap

Suppose in a given year the actual market index goes up 15 percent. Does an indexed annuity owner receive this full amount? Not likely, because in some shape or form, the contract owner is typically going to give up a portion of that gain. When entering into an indexed annuity contract, one needs to determine not only the index they want to link their money to but also how the potential gains of the index are to be credited. The chart coming up summarizes some of the more common choices found in indexed annuities.

Many folks ask me, What is the best credit method to pick? The answer isn't easy because it depends on a number of factors such as the caps and percentage of participation. Furthermore, the best performance also largely depends on how an index moves during a particular year. That said, on indexed annuity accounts I personally own, I gravitate towards the *participation* method as long as the percentage is reasonable and there's no cap. Lastly, in nearly all contracts, one can often hedge their bet by choosing several crediting methods and not limiting their choice to just one.

Crediting Method[2]	Description
Annual Point-to-point	Measures the full growth of the index on an annual basis. Annual basis is not a calendar year; it's the contract year that typically starts when the account is first funded. Anything up to and below the cap is credited to the account and anything over the cap is not credited. If the index goes down during for the year, 0 percent is credited to the account.
Multi-Year Point-to-Point	Same as annual point-to-point but the index is measured over a longer period of time. Typically, this cap is significantly greater than the annual point-to-point method. It is important to remember that when choosing this method, the owner has to wait for interest to be credited over an extended period of time. Additionally, the account might lose a particular year of gains that would have otherwise been locked in had the annual point-to-point crediting method been selected. During prolonged bull market years, however, gains credited in this type of method could be impressive due to the higher caps these typically offer.
Monthly Point-to-Point Cap	Same as annual point-to-point but the measurement of the index is calculated on a monthly basis. At the end of the year, the company simply adds up the gains and credits the total. Important point: although principal and prior earnings are always safe from market loss, for calculation purposes a monthly loss in an index counts against earnings for that year and this downside is not capped For example, one bad

[2] Remember: the account owner is usually making a selection for the following year. At the end of the contract year, the account owner will most often have a window of opportunity to change the crediting method for the following year.

	month where an index loses 5 percent would wipe out five consecutive months of 1 percent gains. Great for strong bull markets, not so great during volatile markets.
Monthly Average	In this crediting method, monthly gains and losses are averaged over the year instead of being added up as with the monthly point-to-point crediting method. Generally more conservative than the monthly point-to-point method but may also reduce returns when compared to a strong market when selecting monthly point-to-point.
Participation Percentage	In this crediting method, an account is credited a percentage of the index gains and is often not subject to a cap. For example, if the chosen index goes up 10 percent and the participation percentage is 80 percent, account will be credited 8 percent.

How Can They Do This?

It may seem like magic how companies can provide market participation but guarantee no losses. If you understand the options markets, you also understand that emulating some aspects of a fixed indexed annuity can be done in a traditional stock brokerage account as well.

First off, remember: money in an indexed annuity is not actually invested in the market. The index is merely acting as a measurement of possible earnings and that's it. If money were actually invested in the index, it would be impossible for anyone to guarantee against loss.

When money resides in an indexed annuity account, in most cases, it's invested in a company's portfolio of investment grade, high quality bonds. These bonds obviously generate interest. The interest generated from these bonds is not kept in the account; rather, it's removed from the bond portfolio and used to purchase a one year stock option on the index the owner selected

For example, suppose

- My account is worth $100,000
- The company's portfolio of bonds generates 4 percent interest ($4,000), and
- I select the S&P 500 as the index linked to my money

The company would then advance my account the $4,000 to be generated from the bonds and uses this

> For curious minds, it should be noted that amongst other reasons, this is why surrender fees are part of an index annuity contract. If one surrenders the policy, the company is protecting the interest they "advanced" the account when purchasing options.

money to buy a one year option on the S&P. On my behalf, this $4,000 is effectively buying the right for the company to control a number of shares on the S&P and after a year credit any potential gains to my account.

As mentioned, when playing the index annuity blackjack game, one is not playing against the house; rather the house is acting as the player's partner. That's because in an indexed annuity, the company is merely *facilitating* the process of investing one's money in investment grade bonds and then using the interest it generates to buy a one-year option on the chosen index.

Furthermore, if at the end of the contract year the index goes up in value, the company continues acting on the owner's behalf by exercising the option. By exercising the option, the potential gains are then credited to the owner's account.

Contrary to some belief, the reason for the cap or limited participation is not because the company keeps gains above these limits. Rather, it's because the amount of interest generated from the bonds can purchase only so many options on the index.

In my example, the $4,000 of interest generated from the portfolio of bonds would never buy a full representation of $100,000 actually being invested in the S&P; it only buys a portion of that money being represented by the index. If the interest generated by the portfolio of bonds increases, more money would be available to purchase more options and as such, the caps or participation would very likely increase as well.

For example, suppose the interest generated from the $100,000 bond portfolio increases from 4 to 8 percent. In this case, $8,000 of interest would likely buy double the amount of stock options on the index and therefore, a larger portion of the $100,000 would be represented. In such a case, the caps and/or participation rates would very likely increase as well.

As with many market option strategies, should the value of the index go down for the year, the only loss is the $4,000 used to purchase the options in the first place. In my example, assuming the index goes down for the year, no options are exercised and therefore there's been no gain; the $100,000 balance would remain fully intact in the index annuity account. Assuming the following year I kept my money linked to the index, the company would then repeat the process all over again.

For more information on how indexed annuities work, you may want to check out a short video I created, *Build a Bond Portfolio to Get Market Returns*, (if on an eReader) by

clicking the image below or visiting
www.youtube.com/alanhaft.

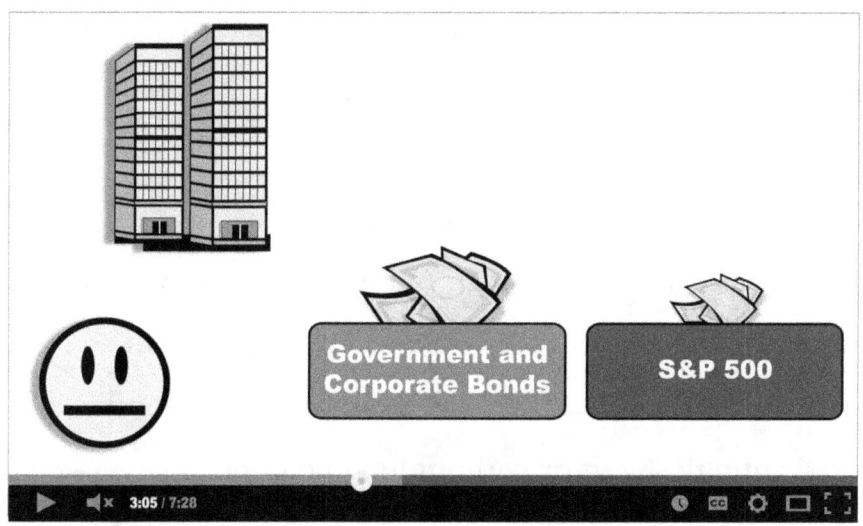

Low Caps

Years ago when interest rates were considerably higher, it wasn't uncommon to see caps and participation rates on indexed annuities significantly greater than where they are in this current historical low interest environment. In many cases, the caps were at least double where they are now.

As a result of this prolonged ultra-low interest rate environment, over the last few years, when evaluating caps and participation rates, although some people liked the idea of no market losses, they didn't like the idea of the low earning potential some of these annuities could produce.

As any financial institution does when looking to attract new accounts, the companies needed to get creative and from that creativity, they developed something called income riders that are now available on many indexed annuity accounts.

An indexed annuity with income riders are often referred to as Hybrid Annuities and perhaps by now, you can understand why there's much misinformation out there. Fixed annuities with variable rates, variable annuities, indexed annuities with or without income riders?

There's no doubt, this is what causes much confusion in the marketplace but congratulations, make it through the rest of my book and chances are, you'll know more than many advisors and news sources do!

Hybrid Annuities and the 7% Guarantee

A hybrid annuity is a term used for indexed annuities that include income rider options, which are available on many indexed annuities.

To illustrate how these riders work, let's start with an example. Suppose I opened a seven-year indexed annuity with a $100,000 single premium. And suppose over the next seven years, I never withdraw any money and suppose—as improbable as it may be—the market index I link my returns to goes down each and every year. As such, my annuity earned no interest. Not so terrible because had I invested in the actual index and it went down seven years in a row, I'd certainly have far less than the $100,000 I started with. But knowing me, I'd still complain about not making any money.

However, had I opened my account with an income rider attached, my original $100,000 would have compounded by let's say 7 percent each year (some riders compound at a lower or higher rate, I'm using 7 as an example). At the end of the seven years, my income account value would therefore be worth approximately $160,000.

Sound pretty good? It is, but there's a very important point that needs to be emphasized about income rider values. In my example, the $160,000 does not represent a value that I can withdraw all at once. It merely represents a value that is used to calculate how much income the account will provide me.

Recall in my extreme example that the index went down each year over the seven year period and I ended up with my initial $100,000 less fees. This represents the *accumulation* or *contract value* of the account. Because I now completed the seven year term, if I contact the company and asked them to close the account and send me all my money at once, they would send me this $100,000 contract value less fees.

But if I instruct the company to send me income from the account, this is where the income value of $160,000 becomes of significant benefit to me.

Depending upon my age, the company will use this higher value to calculate how much income I can receive from the account. It should be noted that *before* one enters into a hybrid annuity, there is almost always an illustration available that shows exactly how much the income rider value will grow each and every year and how much *income* is guaranteed to be generated from the values. As one would see in an illustration, similar to an immediate annuity, the older one is, the greater the amount of income they can expect to receive.

Furthermore, similar to an immediate annuity, it will provide income for life but with one very significant difference: with an immediate annuity, I only have access to the income the immediate annuity produces, not the principal. But when receiving money from an income rider account, *I still retain full access to my account balance.* Additionally, as opposed to an immediate annuity where once the income starts its irrevocable, income from an income rider account can start and stop at any time.

As with any financial vehicle, withdrawals will reduce the balance of my account and if earnings are not enough to replace the withdrawal, this balance would be reduced.

Over an extended period of time, this could reduce the $100,000 account balance essentially down to nothing and as improbable as that is, should it actually happen, the income from the rider will continue for the rest of my life and my spouse's (if elected). If the owner of the account passes away the beneficiaries get whatever's left in the account balance.

Strategies with Income Riders

Some people are attracted to hybrid annuities because they like the idea of placing money in an account where:

- They know their principal is safe from market loss
- Their income account is guaranteed to grow and
- They know exactly much income the account will provide at any point in the future

To illustrate how and where these hybrid annuities might be effective, suppose a fifty-eight-year-old person looking to grow their money and later draw income from it is thinking about where to invest their money: in a market portfolio of stocks and bonds or contributing it into a hybrid annuity.

In the hypothetical market investment approach:

- This person invests $100,000 into a portfolio of stocks and bonds over a ten-year period of time.
- Assuming the portfolio returns 7 percent each year, suffers no market losses and, costs this investor an advisor and/or mutual fund annual fee of one-and-a-half percent, at the end of ten years, the account would be worth approximately $170,000.

To determine the amount of income the account could be expected to produce, assume a withdrawal rate of 4 percent. The income the account would therefore be projected to produce would be roughly $7,000.

Comparing the same hypothetical scenario against using a hybrid annuity:

On an illustration I ran with one particular company, this same person contributes the same amount of money ($100,000) into a hybrid annuity and is guaranteed to receive 6.75 percent per year growth on the income rider value, and earns a 10 percent bonus when opening the account.

At the end of the tenth year, the income rider shows a guaranteed value of $211,383. When initiating the income rider, for this particular person, the account guarantees a

> This withdrawal rate is the most income that can be taken from an account without running out of it. When the concept was conceived, the answer was 4 percent of the account balance but due to market volatility and people living longer, many analysts have adjusted the withdrawal rate to 3 percent.

lifetime annual income of $10,569, representing a 50 percent increase in income over the amount the brokerage account is *projected* but *not guaranteed* to produce.

In order for a portfolio of stocks and bonds over the same period of time to generate the same amount of income using a 4 percent withdrawal rate, the portfolio would need to earn annual returns of approximately 12 percent *each year*. That would not only necessitate incredible luck but also being fully invested in stocks, which is not something people close to or in retirement would ever or should ever do. By using the guarantees provided by the income rider account, there would be no speculation or uncertainty of the future result.

Am I making it seem as if the hybrid annuity is a better approach? No way. Not a chance. The better approach is always going to be determined by a person's unique and very personal needs, financial situation and other factors not mentioned here. So please, by no means take my hypothetical example as something that is construing one approach as better than the other.

To each his own, and the *only* way to determine the best road to travel is not by reading it here or looking up *any* product on the internet but by working with a qualified advisor that can assist in weighing the pros and cons of all possible directions to travel. I'll address this critical point more in the final section of the book.

Fees

When using a hybrid annuity, the rider will cost an annual fee that is generally 0.4 percent and up. In most annuity contracts, this fee is deducted from the account value, not the income rider value. I cannot emphasize enough the importance of this point: in some rare cases, the cost of the rider is a percentage of the income rider value, not the account balance. In nearly all cases, stay away from contracts that calculate it as such!

In most cases, if an income rider is guaranteeing an annual return of let's say 7 percent return, the growth on the income rider value is 7 percent net compounded each year, not 7 percent minus the fee.

Long Term Care and Income Riders

Some hybrid annuities significantly increase the amount of income generated if long term care assistance is needed and verified.

Some contracts will double the amount of income but as with anything discussed in this handbook, details will vary amongst all contacts.

Bonuses

One of the earliest memories I have was when my mom used to take me to the local bank. Those days, when opening new accounts the banks gave away promotional items such as toaster ovens and toys. Thanks to my mom's good heart, she'd load me in the car and take me there whenever opening an account. Even though it might have been March, for me it may as well been Christmas day. She'd do the paperwork and I'd get the toys. What could be better than that?

These days, as an incentive for people to open accounts, companies aren't giving away blenders, china, or toy trucks but many do offer something called "bonus incentives" and there's no doubt these can be quite attractive.

A bonus is simply money added into an account upon funding it and they generally range from around 3 percent upwards to 10 percent or more. So suppose I contribute $50,000 into my annuity, and the annuity pays an 8 percent bonus of $4,000. My opening account balance would therefore start at $54,000 and it then compounds interest off this amount.

Probably sounds good and you'd take it, right? Maybe you shouldn't.

First off, taking a bonus typically means the account owner is electing a longer term contract. While to some this is perfectly acceptable, to others it might not be. In addition, in some cases, taking a bonus could reduce the caps and/or participation percentage rates on index annuities. Always compare!

Furthermore, when it comes to income riders,

> Bonuses are available on many variable annuities as well.

bonuses can sometimes result in lower guaranteed income to the account owner. When comparing income riders with some of the people I've assisted, we've literally seen contracts with no bonus and a 7 percent income rider provide more guaranteed income to an account owner when compared to a contract with a 10 percent bonus and an 8 percent income rider.

The bottom line should be obvious: bonuses can provide some strong benefits to an account but do not judge the benefits of the account just by the bonus itself. One must consider all aspects of the contract and if you are not being advised as such, my advice to you is… walk away!

Vesting

In many cases, bonuses vest over time. If one surrenders the contract before the term is complete, they'll typically return a percentage of the bonus. It isn't uncommon to see a bonus fully vest only upon completion of the term.

In nearly all cases, the contract value will immediately compound interest off the full bonus and mathematically, this most certainly does provide a benefit. However, just keep in mind that in most cases, the account owner doesn't own the full bonus until it is the term is complete.

Using Bonuses in 1035 Exchanges

A 1035 exchange is the provision of the IRS tax code that allows an annuity owner with after-tax money to transfer their account from one annuity to another without tax consequences. The following exchanges of insurance contracts are considered tax-free by the IRS:

- Replacing one annuity contract for another annuity contract with identical annuitants (the person(s) who receives the benefit of the contract)
- Replacing one life insurance policy for another life insurance policy, endowment policy or annuity contract
- Replacing one endowment policy for an identical endowment policy or an annuity contract

It's critical to keep in mind that in order to qualify for a tax-free exchange, the annuity proceeds must be *directly* transferred from one company to the other. With a non-qualified annuity, you will lose the 1035 tax-free status and pay taxes on the earnings if you take possession of the funds and then use them to fund another annuity. Unless the error is caught right away, in most cases, this error cannot be undone and taxes on earnings will be incurred!

Annuities funded with IRA (before tax) money are a different animal. With IRAs, if one takes possession of the money, they can open another IRA account without tax consequence as long as it's done within fifty days (it's actually sixty days but I often jokingly tell people it's fifty to avoid any problems). As with any tax situation, before doing anything, always consult your CPA first.

Exchanging One Annuity for Another

At some point during the term, an owner might want to exchange their annuity for another. This might be in the best interest of the account owner for any number of reasons such as

> 1035 exchanges are available for variable annuities as well, not just fixed annuities.

finding an annuity with a higher rate, and/or finding an annuity with benefits that don't exist on the current contract, such as income riders. But some account owners refrain from doing so given the surrender fees and losses they'd incur if terminating their current annuity prior to the end of the term.

This is where bonuses can be of help. For example, suppose: my current fixed annuity is valued at $50,000, it's paying a fixed rate of 4 percent, and I'm still within the term of the contract. I come across a fixed annuity with a fixed rate of 6 percent and one that also pays an 8 percent bonus. After closely evaluating all aspects of the annuity, I decide it's a better place for my money.

If I surrender my current annuity to exchange it for the new one, I'd have to pay a surrender fee of $3,000 but when adding the new annuity's bonus to the $47,000 from my current annuity, the new annuity's value will immediately increase to $50,760; an amount greater than the $50,000 I had. When it's all said and done:

- I paid no taxes on the exchange due to the 1035 IRS provision,
- Although I paid a surrender fee of $3,000 when breaking the contract of the current annuity, the bonus on the new annuity off-set that loss. I didn't lose anything, I actually gained a little, and,
- My money is now earning a higher rate of return

However, there is one possible negative of the exchange that must be addressed: by exchanging my current annuity for a new one I am re-setting the contract term. To some this might be perfectly fine but to others, starting a new annuity and extending the amount of years they have to hold their contract may not be a wise thing to do.

When exchanging annuities it is important to both evaluate the new contract's features and take time to update and re-evaluate all of one's personal needs such as liquidity and other factors. Also, talk to your CPA before jumping to a 1035 exchange. In many cases, the surrender fee could be a tax deduction for you. In such a case, a tax-free direct transfer into another annuity through a 1035 exchange might not outweigh the benefit of the tax deduction.

Remember: as with any financial decision, always think before you act. After all, taking a breath, pausing to evaluate a decision, and double checking one's intentions is always a sound recipe for success.

Death Benefits

Lastly, another important point to mention about fixed annuities is that in most cases, if one is still within the contract term/surrender period of a contract, upon death most annuities will pass the full account value to heirs without penalty.

Be advised, however, that some annuity contracts will require beneficiaries to receive the remaining account balance over an extended period of time. Should a beneficiary need or want the full contract balance at once, in some cases, they could be faced with penalties.

VARIABLE ANNUITIES

Variable annuities are sometimes confused with a fixed annuity with a variable rate but don't let the similar names confuse you. This is an entirely different annuity with which you can either make a lot of money or lose it. People invest in variable annuities for several reasons including:

- Potential market gains
- Tax deferred investing
- Guaranteed income
- Living benefits
- Death benefits

A key distinguishing attribute of variable annuities is that when funding it, one is investing their money into something called *sub accounts* better known to the public as mutual funds.

Potential Market Gains

When funding a variable annuity, the owner is investing directly in stock and/or bond mutual funds of their choice. Most variable annuities have a large selection of funds to choose from and if an investor doesn't want to select the funds themselves, many variable annuities provide pre-packaged groups of funds for investors' individuals needs and wants: growth, aggressive growth, conservative allocations, or other.

When investing in mutual funds, one has to accept the thrill of victory and the agony of defeat. From one year to the next, gains and/or losses will occur!

Guaranteed Income

As you may recall, a deferred annuity such as a variable annuity simply means that the account owner is initially accumulating money and then potentially converting it to immediate annuity income or annuitization. Annuitizing a deferred annuity such as a variable into an income stream is rarely required; it is merely an option one has as the owner of the account.

Living Benefits

The concept of a living benefit is somewhat similar to income riders found in indexed annuities in that the initial premium is guaranteed to grow by a percentage each year. Just like the income riders on indexed annuities, this "roll up" value is merely a value used to determine the amount of income that can be generated from the account; in most cases, it is not a value that can be withdrawn all at once. The primary benefit living benefits provide is that if the account value drops, the owner has some comfort in knowing that in some shape or form, their income is protected.

There are several types of living benefits available with variable annuities but generally, the living benefit value represents one of two possibilities:

> • **Income for life:** the owner of the contract can annuitize the living benefit value (convert it to an immediate annuity) to create income for life and a spouse as well, if elected.

> • **Withdrawal benefit:** commonly referred to as a guaranteed minimum withdrawal benefit, this income value does not provide income for life, rather, it represents an amount that can be withdrawn over a period of time, typically twenty years or less.

The Ratchet or Step Up

A compelling feature of many living benefits is that if the mutual fund account value exceeds the guaranteed living benefit roll up value, the contract will look back and step the living benefit up to the higher of these two values.

As an example, suppose my account is worth $100,000 and I have a living benefit roll up guarantee of 5 percent per year. Let's also suppose that half-way through the year the value of the account skyrockets to $120,000 but later in the year the account takes a nose and ends up with $90,000. In such a case, some living benefits will look back and determine which of the two values are greater:

- The 5 percent guaranteed roll up value of $105,000, or

- The account value of $120,000

In this case, even though the account value is now less than $120,000, during the year it did at one point exceed the roll up, so in this case, the living benefit would then ratchet, or step up to the $120,000 value. Once stepped up, the $120,000 would then earn the 5 percent roll up, and the look-back process would continue into the next year. Some living benefits step up on a quarterly basis, some do it on an annual basis, and there's even some that have done it on a daily basis.

Be aware: Withdrawals from an account will affect the living benefit value on a dollar-for-dollar or pro rata basis.

> **Dollar-for-Dollar:** In this structure, the living benefit value is reduced by the amount withdrawn from the account. In most cases, this is the ideal method of calculation.
>
> **Pro rata:** in this structure, the living benefit value is reduced by the percentage of the account value taken. Typically, when compared to a dollar for dollar calculation, a pro rata calculation will cause

greater possible reductions to the living benefit value.

Always call the company to make sure you understand how the living benefit value will adjust when money is withdrawn. In some cases, failure to understand so could cause the value to erode and that's obviously not something you want to do.

Death Benefits

The death benefit of a variable annuity simply refers to the amount of money paid to heirs upon one's demise. Death benefits are determined in a number of ways including:

> • **Standard**: the account value (value of mutual funds) is transferred to heirs upon death.
>
> • **Enhanced death benefits such as the roll up and/or ratchet:** these types of death benefits are similar to the living benefit but with these enhancement options, the value isn't used to determine income, it's used to determine the amount that will be passed to heirs in one of the following ways:

- **Roll up:** the initial premium is guaranteed to grow by a certain percentage each year.
- **Ratchet/Step-up:** the value passed to heirs will be the highest account value recorded on an annual or quarterly basis.
- **Roll-up and Ratchet:** as the name implies, the death benefit will be the greater of the roll up percentage or the account value.

Similar to the living benefit, withdrawals from an account will affect the value of the death benefit on a dollar-for-dollar or pro rata basis. Before the first withdrawal—or better yet, before an annuity is opened—be sure to understand how both the living and death benefit values will be effected when withdrawals are taken.

In most cases, regardless if one is still in the surrender period of the contract, variable annuities will typically pay the full account value at death without penalty. Some contracts, however, will require beneficiaries to receive the death benefit over a period of time such as five years or longer. In this case, should they request the contract value all at once, they could be subjected to penalties.

Fees

Have you ever heard that annuities have high fees? If you've heard or read this, whether the source knew it or not, chances are they were referring to variable annuities. Indeed, some variable annuities can be quite costly but there are some newer contracts that have reasonable fees, so please, as with anything in this book, don't ever take any generalization to heart.

On the costly side of some variable annuities, it's not uncommon to see the total cost of ownership include fees consisting of any or all of the following:

- Base contract fee
- Mortality and expense fee (M&E fees)
- Mutual fund fees

If elected, optional rider fees can include:

- Living benefit fees
- Enhanced death benefit fees

On contracts that include some of the above features, I've seen total cost of ownership as high as 4 percent or even greater. Keep in mind, however, the fees amongst products will differ. Regardless if it's an annuity, mutual fund, or other, always be sure to know the total cost of ownership before entering into any financial product.

Understanding Annuities: Six Essentials

While there are many factors that should go into any financial decision you make, when it comes to annuities, I've tried narrowing it down what I believe are six essentials everyone should keep in mind when evaluating products.

1. Understand the type of annuity being evaluated

Immediate annuities: single deposit, income for life.

Fixed annuity with a guaranteed rate: an interest rate that won't change during the duration of the contract term.

Fixed annuity with a variable rate: an interest rate that will change during the contract term.

Fixed annuity with an index rate (fixed indexed annuity): interest rates are linked to various market indexes and are often subjected to a cap or participation rate.

Hybrid annuity: index annuity with an income rider attached.

Variable annuity: performance of sub account mutual funds determine whether or not one earns or loses money.

2. Understand the term of the contract

Be sure to know how many years one is signing up for and the penalties for early surrender. If a market value adjustment provision is in the contract, recognize this adjustment could cause the surrender penalty amount to be more or less than the scheduled amount. I am a firm believer that with the exception of a rare, unforeseen major event, the only reason a contract had to be surrendered was because the owner and/or advisor made "the worst mistake" some annuity owners make that will be addressed in the final important section of this book.

3. Understand the liquidity of the contract

Understand how one can access their money. Return of premium? Ten percent per year? Cumulative penalty-free withdrawals? Contracts will differ.

4. Understand the fees

Be sure to know the total cost of owning the annuity. These fees differ from surrender fees in that these are annual fees incurred while holding the annuity.

Immediate annuities: no fee.

Fixed annuity with a guaranteed rate: typically no fees

Fixed annuity with a variable rate: typically no fees

Fixed indexed annuity: typically no fees

Hybrid annuity (indexed annuity with income rider): Fees typically start at 0.4 percent, upwards to one percent or in some cases, higher

Variable annuity: Fees typically start at around 2.5 percent and upwards to 4 percent or when many optional riders are selected it could be more

5. Understand the ratings of the company: companies to stay away from

Although guarantees provided by insurance companies are known to be the strongest in the financial world, it is still essential to know the rating of the company you're placing money with. In the rare case an insurance company actually goes under, there are various protections in place to back up all or a portion of an owner's account but regardless, one should research the ratings of the company they're considering. Be sure to check ratings with the two de facto rating agencies: AM Best (ambest.com) and Standard and Poor's (standardandpoors.com).

Generally, stick with companies that have at least an A-rating or better. On occasion, there might be a company with a product a notch down from an A rating that might be worth considering only if the product has a highly unique benefit that cannot be found anywhere else. Other than this rare circumstance, I personally stay away from companies with anything less than an A rating.

6. Understand where the annuity fits into your retirement income plan

For reasons soon expressed, this essential is for certain the number one on the list; I just peg it at number six here so that it is not forgotten in the list.

I'll explain the importance of this in the final section of this book.

WHY SOME ADVISORS MIGHT BE AGAINST ANNUITIES

When making an investment into a product, would you rather pay the advisor $6,000 or $1,650? Ridiculous question, right?

Not always.

When evaluating product and choices one can make with their money, there could very well be any number of very valid reasons why some advisors including myself steer their clients far away from annuities such as:

- Other financial products providing a better match to their needs
- Liquidity issues and penalties for early surrender
- Fees
- Tax considerations

There's no doubt that any of the above could be reasons for an individual not to enter into an annuity. But when it comes to annuities, I have often read or heard that annuities have high commissions and to me this immediately implies an advisor is merely suggesting the product only because of the fee it earns them. While it's completely true that some annuities can and do earn what can easily be perceived as high commissions, I firmly believe a very important question needs to then be asked: compared to what?

As a licensed insurance agent, I can earn a commission on an annuity but I'm also a registered investment advisor (RIA). RIAs earn fees not by commissions but either by charging an hourly fixed amount or as percentage based on the amount of assets they are managing, typically in a brokerage account.

Personally, I like the fact that I can earn a fee using one or a combination of both. I find it levels the playing field, helps people understand the choices they have, and if the way I earn a living is a key decision in the products they choose, it gives people plenty of options as to how I can be compensated for my time.

Standard industry fees for managing and overseeing a brokerage account often range from about 1 to 2 percent of the account value each year. So suppose a fee-based advisor such as myself is overseeing and managing a brokerage account that is initially valued at $100,000 and they charge a 1.5 percent fee (as mentioned, RIA fees are typically between 1 and 2 percent, here, I'm just cutting it right down the middle).

In the first year, with some growth, one and a half percent on $100,000 equates to paying the advisor $1,605.[3]

In addition, if one uses a product such as mutual funds in their account, they are going to incur *additional* fees within these investments as well. The average cost of mutual funds in this country are around 1.5 percent, so in my example I'll use *lower cost funds* coming in at 1 percent.

As the brokerage account hopefully grows in value, so does the fee paid to the advisor and the funds. In the table that follows, assuming a hypothetical 7 percent return, one can see the fees increase along with the account balance:

YEAR	VALUE	END YEAR	1.5% ADVISOR FEE	1% FUND FEE	TOTAL FEE
1	100,000	107,000	1,605	1,070	2,675
2	105,395	112,773	1,692	1,128	2,819
3	111,081	118,857	1,783	1,189	2,971
4	117,074	125,269	1,870	1,253	3,132
5	123,390	132,027	1,980	1,320	3,301
6	130,047	139,150	2,087	1,392	3,479
7	137,063	146,657	2,200	1,467	3,666
8	144,457	154,570	2,319	1,546	3,864
9	152,251	162,909	2,444	1,629	4,073
10	160,465	171,697	2,575	1,717	4,292
		TOTALS:	20,564	13,709	34,273

---

[3] In this example the full fee is taken at the end of the year. In many cases, advisors take their fees out on a quarterly basis.

On the contrary, when using an annuity a commission to the advisor generally ranges from around 3 percent or more. Furthermore, it should be noted that the commission is paid not out of the owner's principal but rather, directly from the company to the advisor recommending the product.

Using the $100,000 example, if one placed this amount into an annuity that paid the advisor a higher commission of say 6 percent ($6,000), the fee is indeed initially higher, but over time the fees paid to a fee-based advisor may start out lower but they gradually increase to a greater extent.

In the hypothetical brokerage example above, around the fifth year, the fee-based advisor earns as much as the commissioned advisor initially did but beyond that point, fees paid to the fee-based advisor and the costs to the client are greater.

So, in such an example above, the high commission may wind up earning the commissioned advisor considerably less when compared to the alternative.

That said, first and foremost, I firmly believe the most important factor in any financial decision should be whether or not the product is in a person's best interest.

Once that is determined, then other factors such as fees should be considered into the decision making process but not be the driver of the decision itself.

As with any decision, looking at both the big and small picture and comparing it to the alternatives often leads to the most prudent course of action.

Tax Deferred, Tax Free and No Market Loss

The concept of tax deferral can be very compelling and it's sometimes the reason an annuity is funded in the first place. But for the majority of annuity owners I've talked with, first and foremost it's the features and benefits annuities provide that compelled them to initiate an annuity, not the tax deferred treatment these products provide. The account hopefully grows and interest compounds but this is exactly where the downsides of tax deferral could begin in some cases.

Suppose somewhere in my asset mix is $100,000 that needs a home and I'm specifically interested in:

- Reducing tax

- Keeping this money safe from market loss

- Finding a way to get better returns than CDs, money markets, and/or bonds

I research the marketplace and come across a fixed or indexed annuity. After some further evaluation, I like a particular product and fund it with this $100,000. While my money sits there, I'm living off other parts of my portfolio such as interest, capital gains, and dividends. In this example, I really don't need the interest the annuity is generating, so I just leave it there to compound and grow.

Years go by. I still have the annuity. Maybe at some point in the future I take some money out of it and when I do, I don't like it all that much because I'm taxed on the accumulated earnings.

Furthermore, not only am I taxed on the annuity earnings but just like money coming out of an IRA, withdrawals from the annuity caused additional taxes on my social security and I want no part of that.

So years fly by and whether it's because I just want to leave the account to my family or I just want to prevent paying the tax, I just let the annuity sit there and collect more and more deferred interest. Then the day eventually comes that my horrific driving finally does me in.

At the time of my death that indexed annuity's value was around $225,000, which is paid out to my beneficiaries. When it comes time to settle the estate's taxes, in this hypothetical but not uncommon example, the beneficiaries are shocked to learn its real value was only $140,000 after income and some estate taxes are paid.

The $100,000 contribution represents the cost basis and all the earnings piled up over that amount are called deferred earnings, meaning that when the annuity is cashed out or inherited, someone has to pay the piper.

You must realize that when it comes to deferring tax, someone always has to eventually pay the tax and there are a couple things that could have been done differently to meet the original goals of reducing tax, keeping money safe, and participating in market gains.

Far too often, I find advisors and/or investors wishing to reduce tax, keep their money safe and strive for higher returns just jump into an indexed (or other) annuity simply because of the features and benefits they provide. In many cases, their choice was likely the best one they could make.

But if one's goals are similar to benefits provided by an indexed annuity, then a product bearing similar characteristics should not be ignored.

So, suppose for a portion of one's money someone was looking to:

- To keep their money safe *and* participate in market returns…

- Defer taxes on the potential growth of the money….

- ….have access to their money in case they need it, get to it *tax free* and…

- …pass the asset to beneficiaries *tax free as well*

… is there anything out there that can accomplish this? (Hint: it's not an indexed annuity but something close to it).

There's only *one place to get all the above* and it's called an "indexed universal life insurance policy."

Indexed Universal Life (IUL)

When hearing the words "life insurance," people often respond to this suggestion incredulously, "Thanks, but I need something for when I'm alive, not dead."

When I first heard this concept myself, I'm sure I said something to the same effect but having learned a few things about this highly modified type of insurance, I've decided to own several of these policies myself and for some, these products might also provide the a good fit to their asset mix as well.

The perception that life insurance does nothing but cost money and only serves to pay someone a bunch of money when they're gone is just simply an outdated definition of insurance. Things with insurance have changed quite a bit and IULs are a relatively new beast on the block. This type of highly modified insurance has benefits to an insured while they're alive, not only when they're dead.

When properly designed this type of modified life insurance could provide some compelling features while one is alive including such as:

- Market participation without downside risk (in most IULs the caps are significantly greater when compared to indexed annuities)
- The ability to borrow money that's been accumulated in the policy tax-free
- When one passes, beneficiaries receive the asset tax-free instead of taxable (as with annuities)
- If elected, a long term care benefit that can be drawn off the death benefit

One company's example returns follow. Note that 0 percent interest was credited when the S&P 500 went down for the year. It's on these occasions the account balance would not decline due to market performance. Caps and participation will differ depending on the company and the year in which interest is credited.

Date	S&P 500 Index Growth	Interest Credited	Date	S&P 500 Index Growth	Interest Credited
12/20/79	14.31%	14.00%	12/15/94	-1.73%	0.00%
12/18/80	22.85%	14.00%	12/14/95	35.49%	14.00%
12/17/81	-7.43%	0.00%	12/19/96	20.88%	14.00%
12/16/82	9.89%	13.85%	12/18/97	28.10%	14.00%
12/15/83	19.48%	14.00%	12/17/98	23.52%	14.00%
12/20/84	2.92%	4.09%	12/16/99	20.24%	14.00%
12/19/85	26.23%	14.00%	12/14/00	-5.49%	0.00%
12/18/86	17.50%	14.00%	12/20/01	-14.99%	0.00%
12/17/87	1.54%	0.00%	12/19/02	-22.43%	0.00%
12/15/88	12.88%	14.00%	12/18/03	23.18%	14.00%
12/14/89	27.95%	14.00%	12/16/04	10.47%	14.00%
12/20/90	-5.93%	0.00%	12/15/05	5.63%	7.88%
12/19/91	15.87%	14.00%	12/14/06	12.16%	14.00%
12/17/92	13.83%	14.00%	12/20/07	2.43%	3.40%
12/16/93	6.41%	8.97%	12/18/08	-39.37%	0.00%
			AVERAGE	7.73%	9.03%

To accomplish the above bullet pointed goals and make it compelling enough, the policy has to be properly designed relative to the individual and their specific needs. There is no template or cookie cutter policy that is one-size-fits-all. It must be tailored to you.

That said, the general rule of thumb when designing these type of policies is, the greater the death benefit, the greater the cost of insurance and therefore the less cash being accumulated within the policy due to the cost of insurance.

Remember that! because when and if an insurance policy is properly designed with the least amount of death benefit, the benefits to the insured *while they are alive* can be compelling, such as:

- Defer tax
- Accumulate money safe from market loss
- Participate in market returns without market risk
- Lock in their account value each year
- Borrow money out tax-free and
- Pass the asset to beneficiaries tax-free

Example of a Properly Designed IUL

First off, if you've read this book from the beginning, you'll know I'll preface this with one important point: coming up I'll discuss what a "properly designed" policy could look like **but**…. only when one's personal situation and goals are truly known, a "properly designed" insurance policy might wind looking far different than the one I'm going to describe.

Furthermore, depending on the individual's needs, the concept might wind up being:

- Something I would not recommend when fully understanding one's specific needs and financial situation,
- It might wind up being something one simply *cannot*

do due to very poor health, and/or,

- The policy design might wind up being a significant deviance from my version of a "properly constructed designed policy" I'm going to outline coming up.

I've said it once so I'll say it again… only when knowing one's personal situation can *anything* be deemed "properly designed" or an efficient use of one's money.

OK, enough said.

When discussing IULs and the benefit it could provide a person while they're alive, I often show two illustrations to demonstrate the difference between a policy designed for building up as much cash as possible and one that isn't designed as efficiently.

The illustrations I often have at my fingertips show the following:

- The same exact person (age, health, etc.)…
- Contributing the same exact of money over the same exact period of time…
- Earning the same exact amount of interest on their money

I then show that further down the road:

- One illustration is protected to have nearly **double** the amount of cash for the person while they're alive when compared to the other.

Nearly **double** the amount of cash! when compared to the other and remember: this was comparing:

- The same person contributing the same exact amount,

- Over the same exact period of time and...

- ....earning the same amount of interest.

How can that be? Any idea?

It's because of the design with *double* the amount of cash for the owner to withdraw has nearly *half* the amount of death benefit compared to the other!

To keep it simple: the hard and fast rule when designing these types of policies is that the greater the death benefit, the greater *the cost* of insurance and therefore, the *less cash* being built up due to the cost of insurance.

Remember that! Because *when* and *if* an insurance policy is properly designed with the ***least amount of death benefit***, the benefits to the insured *while they are alive* can be compelling.

Compelling enough to some to satisfy the desire to defer tax, accumulate money safe from market loss, participate in market returns without market risk, lock in the account value each year, borrow money out **tax free** *and* pass the asset to beneficiaries **tax free**.

The Least Amount of Insurance

Designing a policy with least amount of insurance is not something determined by me, another advisor, or the insurance company. It's something determined by the IRS. In order for a policy to provide the above, it must have a minimum amount of life insurance attached to it. In the past, people loaded up on these to take advantage of the tax-free aspects of the money being contributed into them but the IRS later reduced the amount that can be contributed and now base the allowable amount primarily on:

- The age of the insured
- The amount they plan to contribute each year
- The projected returns, and other factors not mentioned here

As long as there's a minimum amount of insurance, the IRS allows for tax-deferral as well as tax-free borrowing against the policy as well as passing the asset to beneficiaries tax-free.

Hey! Borrowing Costs Something!

It sure does. But hold on, because there's some important points to note here.

When borrowing money tax-free, it's done by borrowing against the asset itself. This is the reason it can be taken tax-free and it's not dissimilar from borrowing against other assets such as the equity in one's house where that too can be borrowed out tax-free. However, when borrowing equity from a house, one pays the interest cost, typically on a monthly basis.

Borrowing equity from an insurance policy is where death actually serves the insured because at death, the interest owed on the built up loan costs are simply deducted from the insurance amount being passed to heirs.

Policy illustrations show this and yes, in the past if too much money was borrowed and too much interest costs were built up, policies could and did implode. And when they did it was nuclear. Limbs, hearts, and other body parts were indeed lost because of the retroactive taxes policy owners faced.

These days, however, nearly all policies now have guarantees against this taking place. The protection is typically called something like *over-loan protection*, which simply guarantees that the policy cannot cause retroactive taxation if there's been too much money borrowed from a poor performing policy.

If a policy is headed that way, with over loan protection in place, the company won't allow for additional borrowing to take place that could negatively impact the owner. Furthermore, an experienced advisor will point out the many exits an owner can take from a policy should interest costs grow too high.

Potential Downsides

Is an IUL policy for everyone?

No way.

Most importantly, I would not recommend any IUL concept to anyone who needs their money returned in a short period of time. In general, for these types of policies to be considered, they really need to be considered for longer range planning and have time to build up money within them. Just how much time depends on many factors but typically it needs to be *at least* five years.

Also, the wheels on this bus can potentially fall off if an advisor constructs a policy that is designed with a death benefit far above the IRS minimum requirement. If designed this way, the policy fees and costs will soak up too much of the cash build up and not make it very attractive to the person while they are alive.

That said, if a person wants a greater death benefit than the IRS minimum and still wants to have at least some cash available in the policy to

> Interested in learning more about fees and the choices we have? Visit www.youtube.com/alanhaft and check out the short animated video I created on the subject entitled "The effect of fees on your money"

borrow against, then a policy with a higher death benefit should not be construed as one that is poorly designed. But again, if a person's desire is to have as much cash build up as possible, then designing the policy with anything greater than the minimum requirement is serving only to cost the owner higher fees, and that's obviously not a good thing.

The final potential disadvantage I'll discuss here has nothing to do with the company, fees, performance, and advisors who fail to construct the most efficient plan. It is due to user error. Although rare, I've seen some people enter into a properly designed policy and simply stop making any sort of contribution into it. If contributions were a part of a plan and they are not made, then the costs can erode whatever cash is in the policy over time. When that happens, it would obviously defeat the purpose of having taken out the policy in the first place.

Needless to say, this is no different with any plan. If one were to plan on having a certain amount of money in, for example, a 401(k) at retirement and they simply stop making contributions, the account would obviously not achieve the intended results.

Note: I've used the terminology 'planned contributions' into an insurance-based plan over time. It's also possible to make a single contribution and simply let the money grow from there. The aspects and outcome of this method are beyond a book about annuities but just be aware that single contributions can be made.

If you already own an annuity and having read the last section and are concerned with the tax treatment of distributions to you and/or your beneficiaries, the very first thing to do is speak to a person qualified to address your potential outcomes. Perhaps your fear is unwarranted and there's nothing to be concerned about, or perhaps there's most definitely room for improvement.

For Those Concerned with Taxation to Them

If one is concerned with the amount of taxes they'll pay when deferred interest is taken from a non-qualified annuity—an annuity was funded with money that has already been taxed—there are a few possible choices one might have to minimize the tax.

> **Annuitize it:** as a reminder, annuitizing means converting the annuity balance into income for life. Annuitizing a policy funded with non-qualified money results in income that initially has tax favorable treatment due to the annuity exclusion ratio rule. (See the section on immediate annuities for more details.)

> **Cash out of it:** Re-allocate the money into a financial product that provides tax advantaged Income. Sound nuts? Not always. In some cases, this

could make sense. One must very carefully weigh the after tax amount against the benefits a new investment could provide such as a tax-free muni bond. Actually doing such a thing depends on many factors such as possible penalties if still within the term of the contract, risks in alternative financial products and other factors not mentioned here. Also keep in mind that if a loss is taken due to a penalty, it could be a tax deduction as well. Speak to your CPA first!

Don't worry about it: Perhaps you have tax deductions and/or write-offs to take against the taxes owed when money is taken from an annuity. I've come across people who were concerned with taking a distribution from a tax standpoint but after I advised them to first speak to a CPA in some cases they were pleasantly surprised to hear the taxes they'd face weren't nearly as impactful as they initially feared and as such, the best of all choices wound up being to...

Leave it: leaving it alone is sometimes the best choice above all.

For Those Concerned with Taxation to Their Heirs

If one is concerned with the amount of taxes beneficiaries will face when their non-qualified annuities are passed to heirs, let's look at choices this type of person has.

Let's start with an example. Suppose a seventy-year-old woman has an annuity worth $200,000, which was funded with after-tax non-qualified money of $100,000, so she has $100,000 in deferred interest that is fully taxable to her beneficiary.

If she dies, then her beneficiaries will incur ordinary income tax on the $100,000 deferred interest and in addition, they might incur estate tax as well.

If this woman dies when she is eighty-eight, assuming the annuity earned an average of 5 percent and her beneficiaries were faced with a combined 40 percent tax, the inheritance could incur approximately $126,314 of income tax. Additional estate taxes might apply as well.

Recognizing this, she has a few options as to how she can manage the taxes for her heirs, such as:

- **Leave it:** just leave it alone and let the kids deal with it (some people are perfectly fine with this approach).

- **Take from it:** take small distributions from the annuity and use these distributions to fund an insurance policy (or other) that has a death benefit enough to pay the projected taxes that will be owed on interest at death.

- **Annuitize it:** annuitize the annuity (convert it into an immediate annuity) and use all or portions of the proceeds to fund an insurance policy. (See section on immediate annuities).

- **Terminate it:** terminate the annuity, cash out, pay the tax, and use the net proceeds to fund an insurance policy.

If she has no plans to ever use the annuity and it's destined to beneficiaries, **termination** might wind up being her best choice.

Suppose after consulting with her CPA to find out exactly how much tax she'd owe, the CPA tells her she'll owe forty percent tax on the distribution ($80,000) and come away with $120,000.

Who'd ever want to do that?

If she has no plans to ever use the annuity and it's destined for beneficiaries, it might wind up being her best choice.

For good practice, suppose she takes $20,000 of the $120,000 leftover money after the annuity is cashed out and simply puts it in the bank. This is done for safe measure, in the world of "just in case she need a few dollars" type of thing.

She then takes the $100,000 leftover and uses it to fund an IUL policy.

At her assumed death (88), one company's policy is projected to provide heirs with a **tax free** death benefit of approximately $375,000, which is obviously greater than the $289,471 after-tax money the annuity is projected to leave her beneficiaries at the same point of time.

If she passes sooner, the difference between the two can be even greater.

If she leaves the annuity alone, in order to leave behind same amount of after tax money to heirs, the annuity would have to approximately grow roughly more than an *additional $160,000* in order to achieve around the same result as the insurance policy is projected to provide.

Is this a good plan or not? It depends.

It obviously depends on the intentions of the annuity owner and a variety of other factors.

Bottom line: if you own an annuity and are planning to pass it to heirs, it's wise to have it analyzed by qualified professionals including a CPA to determine what the best plan of action is. In many cases, I've been visited by beneficiaries of annuities asking, "is there anything we can do about the tax we owe?" and in nearly all cases, something could have been done but while the owner was still alive.

CHAPTER NINE: THE SINGLE WORST MISTAKE MANY INCOME INVESTORS MAKE

At this point, you might be thinking any of the above products aren't for you or perhaps they're something you'll to consider as part of your overall asset mix. Should that happen, the next step is to typically find someone who knows these products quite well. The person you meet most likely has the greatest of intentions. If they're good at their job, they'll first do their due diligence and ask a few questions about your needs and goals. Once assessed, it's then they'll likely pick an investment product and discuss its features and benefits. If all looks good, then congratulations, you just found a new something to include as part of your asset mix.

But was the product selected truly the best choice? It might have been but I often find an extra step is needed to truly understand whether or not it was the best fit.

And if this extra step is not taken before *any* product is selected, one could easily find themselves making the single worst mistake not only annuity owners might make but *any* investor selecting product as well.

Before revealing this mistake, allow me to digress for a moment.

The Death of Pensions

A long, long time ago, many people worked at a company their entire careers. At retirement, most people left the company with a pension that for the rest of life ahead took care of their retirement income needs and what a fantastic thing it was.

When it came to figuring out retirement income, all one had to basically do was fill out a form to determine how they wanted to take their pension and whether or not they wanted to include a spouse. From there, their job was quite simple: merely deposit each check every month for the rest of their lives.

All the difficult and complicate decisions as to…

- Where to invest
- How to get the most amount of income
- How to compensate for inflation
- How to ensure one wouldn't run out of money
- How to keep income flowing to a surviving spouse

…were left in the hands of professional actuaries and managers who collectively spent all their time making all these complex decisions for us.

These days, however, things have changed quite a bit. Especially over the last decade, pensions have quickly become a dinosaur of the past. Only a select few still get them and for those that do, governments and corporations are successfully reducing, and in some cases, completely eliminating them.

With rare exception, these days it's not large departments of full time actuaries and managers managing pensions living and breathing this stuff; for the most part it's now us, the individual, who are left to care for their retirement.

When I ask people why this is so, the most common response I hear has to do with low interest rates and market volatility making it difficult for companies to continue shouldering the responsibility of paying out pensions. No doubt, this is part of the reason but the foundation of the reason goes actually goes back long before the period we're now in.

A Baby Is Born

Back in the 70s, civil service and the majority of employees at companies received pensions. At that time, an evolution was also taking place. Up until then, for the most part, when one wanted to invest in the market they did it either by picking individual stocks or hiring a broker to do it for them.

Although some mutual funds existed long before then, it wasn't until the 70s that these investment vehicles just started to flourish. No longer did people have to select individual stocks themselves; thanks to more and more funds coming into the marketplace, one could simply invest with a fund manager who did all the guesswork for them.

Seeking to attract more money into their funds, the mutual fund industry got creative. Companies banded together and lobbied Congress and basically said, although most of the public had pensions at retirement, few had anything in retirement *savings* and what better way to do it than invest in their funds?

What if people wanted to buy a boat? Take a vacation? Take care of unforeseen needs? True, pensions provided lifetime income but they didn't provide opportunities to spend larger lump sum of monies. Congress liked what they heard. After all, inspiring people to save and later spend it would serve to spark the economy for generations to come and furthermore, future taxes on this money would help fund government.

To motivate people to save, Congress basically told the public that for every dollar they saved towards retirement, they'd get a tax deduction and the vehicle conceived to do this in would be in something called a 401(k).

Keep in mind a very significant point: when the 401(k) was conceived, its *sole purpose* was to provide people with a retirement savings to supplement a pension and that's it.

As 401(k)s slowly but surely seeped into the public, companies soon realized they could start doing away with pensions and let the 401(k)s take their place. After all, creating and administering pensions comes with lots of risk, liability, and high costs—something no company likes. So to a major extent, 401(k)s started to replace pensions.

These days, 401(k)s are now being asked to do something they were never designed to do: be the primary source of retirement income. Have you ever determined how much income one can expect to receive from a 401(k)? In nearly all cases, it's far less than what a pension would have provided.

So it's now up to us individuals to do the job that those full time, experienced pension managers once provided. In most cases, retiring simply means retiring from one's job but the work isn't over. In fact, in many cases, it's just begun and this new work is running what I commonly refer to as...

Retirement, Inc.

Think of Retirement, Inc. as your very own retirement company that is basically comprised of the following departments:

- The asset management department: decides where to invest
- The income management department: determines how to get the most income from the investments and make sure one doesn't outlive it.
- The Healthcare Department: responsible for making sure insurance, long term care and other health related issues are addressed.
- The Tax Department: responsible for determining and hopefully reducing tax.
- Estate Planning Department
- Succession planning, and more

Like any good business, projections should be made, cash flow should be analyzed, taxes should be considered, and health issues assessed. In addition, *how* the assets are going to be set up and passed as well as other important aspects of Retirement, Inc. should be factored into just about every financial decision you make.

When selecting *any* financial product, are the above being addressed or are you and/or your advisor merely looking at product in and of itself? A well-run company would not invest in *any* product to support infrastructure without fully assessing its costs and efficiencies in terms of how the product will affect other parts of the company and what it will do to the company's overall bottom line. Perhaps a product on its own looks fantastic but understanding how the product will affect other aspects of the company is as important, if not more important than the product itself.

Likewise, whether it's investing in an annuity, stocks and bonds, or whatever else, you will do yourself an **enormous** service to **first** understand **how** the product fits into the overall framework of Retirement, Inc. Taking a short amount of time to do this will often create magic for your retirement and will often lead to:

- Higher income
- Lower risk
- Lower taxes
- Lower fees
- More money to heirs

Sound good? Maybe. But the next logical question is *how?*

It's actually not too difficult; all you have to do is understand the very important concept of...

The Retirement Roadmap

When I first started in the financial planning industry, I was trained to collect lots of data from a person then put it all into a computer so that a financial blueprint could be provided—a thick book filled with colored pie charts, graphs and a seemingly endless amount of math and fine print. Then I'd meet with the person and review it.

Of all intended outcomes, the one thing that by far prevailed the most was that the clients and I both got dizzy looking at the thing. But there was one part of that book that was somewhat helpful. Somewhere buried in the last section or so were a few pages summarizing assets with a projected growth rate. From these assets, one could project the amount of income they were due to generate. But even though this part of the thick book was helpful, it was filled with just way too much math and was far too cumbersome and complicated for most folks to grasp, let alone actually implement.

These days, I forgo these thick books and heavy-handed reports. Instead, I produce two or three spreadsheet pages by hand and collectively call them a retirement roadmap. Depending on the client's asset mix, some maps might be a page; others might be more complex.

Regardless of the amount of pages, I find the map to be the single most valuable tool I use for my own retirement planning and for those I assist. Best of all, should I go for a drive and end up on a cloud somewhere, everyone I work with has a blueprint of their retirement for the rest of their lives.

The first step in the process is to get a small handful of questions answered. From there, my job is then to lay out the assets along with their projected growth rate dictated and anticipated by the client. This first pass represents the path the individual is currently on and with it in hand, one can then very clearly visualize:

- The estimated growth of their assets over time
- The estimated amount of income that can be expected (or is coming) from these assets
- The taxation on them

• Income from other sources and how it affects the income from the assets

• When and if money will run out

When seeing the map and working with input from others such as a CPA, sometimes the current course of action is as good as it possibly can be with little or no room for improvement. Other times, however, the current course of action reveals an entirely different story such as:

• Estimated growth rates will not produce enough income

• Taxes are decimating the amount of net income one is due to receive (or is receiving)

• For those not yet taking Social Security the plan to take it sooner (or later) is not in their best interest

• Withdrawals from the assets are too high and as a result could cause one to outlive their money

• Assets inherited by heirs will be subject to high tax, etc., etc.

Most importantly for most, the map really shines when it comes to helping pick financial products. By plugging product into the map, I've had people completely change their current course of action because what once seemed as if it was the perfect product quickly became something that didn't serve the best interests of Retirement, Inc..

For example, I've had many married couples come in who have money in cash, are looking to invest it in individual stocks, and want some advice on where to place it. Before any conversation about stocks takes place, I ask how these stocks will affect their Retirement, Inc. Often there's no clear understanding of this. So together we'll develop a retirement roadmap and collectively come to the conclusion that they don't need nearly as much growth on their money as they had initially anticipated. With small modifications to their current course of action, lower returns in more conservative investments combined with a modified structure of how and where they will take their income from not only *increases* their income but it significantly *reduces* the risk required to do the job.

Conversely, I've also had people come to realize that their conservative approach was going to lead them to run out of money. These epiphanies *could not* have been made without first visualizing Retirement, Inc. through a retirement roadmap or something like it.

The bottom line is this: true planning works but for it to really be effective and useful, I've found it also needs to be extremely simple to understand and implement. The Roadmap gives me and those I work with the opportunity to explore the what-ifs without actually doing them yet, such as:

- What if we used this product?
- Will it generate enough income for us?
- What if we used something else?
- Is that guarantee we're paying for really necessary?
- Is that annuity really the best fit?
- Is a seven year annuity contract really too long?
- What happens if we use bonds?
- What if we took income from here instead of over there? Will that increase or reduce or income and taxes?
- What if we took Social Security at age seventy instead of sixty two? Will that help or hurt us? How will we fill that gap?

So, whether using what if scenarios done through a retirement roadmap or something like it, before investing in *any* product of *any* kind, it is critical to first understand just how the product is going to affect other parts of Retirement, Inc.

Failing to take this extra critical step often leads to the single worst mistake some people make with their money: picking a product merely because of the product itself and not selecting a product because of how it fits into the overall framework of Retirement, Inc..

Run your retirement well, treat it as your new company, and before selecting any product whatsoever, do yourself a giant favor: first go through the what-ifs. Through the roadmap, first throw a rock into the water and watch how its ripples effect all areas of the water before diving in.

For me and the many people I've worked with, this is the true secret of financial success.

CONCLUSION

I hope you've learned something from this short book and if you have, an author's greatest compliment is to hear that you passed it to someone else.

If you aren't sure about how to run Retirement Inc., how to create your own retirement roadmap, or you just have some additional questions about income investments or any other investments for that matter, feel free to reach out to me anytime. I've written books and countless articles on virtually every investment under the sun and welcome questions and feedback from my readers so please, don't be shy.

I wish you the best of luck, success, and happiness and may your current or coming retirement truly be the best times of your life.

With regards,

Alan Haft

19800 MacArthur Blvd., Ste. 280

Irvine, CA 92612

800.803.0081

alan@alanhaft.com
Follow me on Twitter @alanhaft

www.ingramcontent.com/pod-product-compliance
Lightning Source LLC
Chambersburg PA
CBHW051631170526
45167CB00001B/140

* 9 7 8 1 4 9 7 5 8 8 2 1 9 *